healing your inner child

healing
your
inner
child

re-parenting yourself for a more secure & loving life

natasha levinger

STERLING ETHOS

New York

STERLING ETHOS
New York

ISBN 978-1-4549-4676-2
ISBN 978-1-4549-4677-9 (e-book)

Library of Congress Control Number: 2022951334

For information about custom editions, special sales, and premium
purchases, please contact specialsales@unionsquareandco.com.

Printed in Canada

2 4 6 8 10 9 7 5 3 1

unionsquareandco.com

Cover and interior illustration by Eiko Ojala
© 2023 Union Square & Co.
Interior design by Kevin Ullrich

Contents

Introduction   ix

Chapter One
**What Is the Inner Child and Why
Should We Get to Know Them?**
1

Chapter Two
Energy Healing
24

Chapter Three
Your Inner Parent
46

Chapter Four
**How Do We Create a Strong,
Loving Inner Parent?**
62

Chapter Five
The Inner Critic
94

Chapter Six
Communicating with Your Inner Child
117

Chapter Seven
Your Higher Self
145

Chapter Eight
**The Inner Child in Relationships:
Boundaries, Codependency, and
Self-Compassion, Oh My!**
162

Chapter Nine
The Inner Child and Narcissist Abuse
180

Chapter Ten
The Joyful Inner Child
198

Acknowledgments   205

Index   207

About the Author   212

To all the younger versions of me and everyone who wasn't believed: I see you, and I believe you.

Introduction

I am writing this book for anyone who needs it, and I'm also writing it for my twenty-one-year-old self. And my six-year-old self. And my fifteen-year-old self. I'm writing this book for all of our inner children who felt like whatever sad, angry, scared, or upsetting feeling they were experiencing in that moment was the absolute complete truth, and that they were alone in it.

As you will learn in this book, our wounded inner child is stuck in the past, where they are lost in their worldview. The inner child's perspective is usually very self-limiting, made up of extreme either/or beliefs ("you're the best" or "you're the worst") and unaware of the adult self that exists in the present. When we merge with the inner child, we get lost in this viewpoint, losing sight of who we really are. We go down a portal like the one in *Alice in Wonderland*—a drop into another world that makes us forget our wholeness and has us thinking we are broken or not enough.

I have been a practicing intuitive reader, medium, energy healer, and inner child healing teacher for a while now, and I have never met anyone who is actually broken. Our true selves are whole, complete, and a great source of love. Maybe they are even love itself. Most of our problems, in my opinion, stem from splitting off from that innately worthy self and forgetting who we really are.

I relate to many of my clients who grew up in homes where their true selves were conditioned out of them. My mother had a dominant, narcissistic personality, and I learned very quickly that my inner compass had to be focused on her or I would suffer the consequences. The consequences in my case looked like anything from emotional abandonment to triangulation to verbal abuse. This left me cut off from my intuition and with an innate feeling that there was something wrong with me.

Children need to establish a feeling of safety within. When our parents are hurting us, we often believe that we are the bad ones in order to retain a feeling of control. But if we imagine that our caregivers are bad, how are we supposed to feel truly secure? It's impossible: we simply cannot hold that knowledge in our hearts and minds. We don't have an inner adult yet. We only have the external adult in front of us. So we then must become the ones at fault. And as you'll learn in a later chapter, we literally don't have the ability to calm our own nervous systems when we are that young.

When this kind of conflict happens, we split from our true, authentic self and develop parts of ourselves that can help us survive in the environment. That looks different for everyone. It can look like developing a part of your personality that is determined to be perfect at all costs, or cutting yourself off from your feelings, or being a bully like your caretaker, or attacking yourself with judgment in order to do it before your parent does, to name a few responses.

We then grow up, and until we learn how to honor and validate our true selves and each create a real inner adult, we will feel our inner children as being as real and alive, as if we were still kids. Learning inner child healing can help you develop that inner adult while also integrating and welcoming your past self with an open heart. By practicing the energy healing techniques outlined in this book, you can get to know your true, expansive nature more and more deeply.

You do not have to have had a traumatic background in order to benefit from inner child healing. We can't compare trauma, and no one has come through childhood without pain. We can also have wounding as adults. And you may have had an incredibly supportive home life but dealt with systemic racism or homophobia, or maybe you grew up in poverty, or you suffered from any number of issues that were out of your control.

All of that is certainly out of our depth to handle when we are children. But when we can learn to experience ourselves as having a center of a loving adult that is validating of our inner child, we can feel more supported, resilient, and capable of handling whatever comes up.

My journey started in 1992 when I discovered inner child healing through my therapist at that time, Margaret Paul. Later I learned energy healing from a teacher who was trained at Psychic Horizons in San Francisco. And more recently I became familiar with Internal Family Systems, which is an amazing modality of therapy that uses inner child work.

The tools I learned that I am sharing with you in this book have given me the ability to care for the versions of myself that still believed the childhood programming stating that they weren't enough and no one cared for them. These tools helped me to find out and connect to who I really am. It's an honor to be able to share them with you.

Author's Note: I have shared some of my clients' experiences in this book. Their names have been changed to protect their privacy.

CHAPTER ONE

What Is the Inner Child and Why Should We Get to Know Them?

The phrase *inner child* is commonly used these days, but it can turn a lot of people off because it may seem too cutesy or vague. You might visualize a version of yourself as a child sitting inside of you, but that's a little . . . weird? And also, how is that helpful? Spoiler alert: It's *incredibly* helpful! (I guess that's not really a spoiler if I've written a whole book about it.) Of all the tools I've shared with my clients and all of the tools I've learned myself, it has been one of the most helpful, if not the most helpful.

The concept of labeling this part of our psyche as the inner child is relatively new. It was originally conceived by Eric Berne, a Canadian psychoanalyst, who called it the "child ego state" in 1940. This means that our ego (our sense of identity) has many different parts, and the inner child is part of it. (So is the inner critic, and even the inner parent.) Although its meaning might seem clear enough at this abstract level, that doesn't give us a sense of what it means to really *feel* it on an intuitive level in a way that allows us to understand what that means for us personally.

So, setting theory aside, the best way I've found to explain it is this: the inner child represents your gut feelings, from the most painful and challenging to the happiest and most creative and joyful ones. The painful ones are coming from the past where your wounded inner child lives, still feeling they are in those past moments. But the happy ones are expressions of who you are in the present, your true self beyond trauma or painful childhood programming.

In the Somatic Experiencing framework, they say that trauma is not the terrible thing that happened to you, but the energy that gets locked in your body as a result of it. So, to use that language, that energy is the inner child. Let's say you were emotionally abandoned frequently in childhood. You weren't able to have the trauma negative feelings resolved because your caretakers weren't capable of doing that. No one came to you and said, "Oh, I'm so sorry that I rejected you. I shouldn't have taken my problems out on you. I love you. I'm here now.

It wasn't your fault." Now, when you experience anything close to abandonment (which could even look like someone withdrawing for reasons having nothing to do with you), that energy of the inner child gets activated, and it feels like childhood abandonment.

You can have multiple wounded inner child parts that are waiting to be rescued by your inner parent, who can let them know "Hey! I'm here! It's the present, and you don't need to stay in that moment any longer. I'm an adult, I'm your caretaker, you are safe."

The gut punch feeling one of my clients felt when she told her brother she was going back to school and he said it sounded like "another one of your pipe dreams" came from a wounded inner child part. Even though she also was feeling his criticism in the moment, the intensity of it came from the past, when she always had to perform perfectly in order to get her mother's approval. (Later, we'll get more into what to do when you are having an appropriate reaction to something happening while simultaneously experiencing an inner child reaction to it. Also known as life.)

But that feeling of glee I feel jumping on a trampoline? That's my free, happy inner child. And *that* is coming from the present joyful moment.

You may have noticed that I used extreme ends of the emotional spectrum to describe what the inner child is feeling, and that is because the feelings associated with your inner child generally are extreme. Real-life children often think in extremes ("this is the *best* day of my life!" or "I hate *everyone!*"), and when we become aware of our inner child, we will notice that kind of language when we talk to ourselves as being an indication that the inner child is in the proverbial house. The inner critic (who is often an inner child part) also uses extreme language like this, and in both cases it's a good way for you to know that the inner parent is definitely not at home.

Throughout this book, when I refer to the inner child, I'm usually referring to the wounded inner child, the one who needs healing. Think of a time you felt rejected, sad, ashamed—any challenging feeling in your adult life. The wounded inner child is the reactionary part of you that is rooted in those unresolved feelings. When we perceive interactions in our lives through the lens of an original, historical wound, that is the perception of the wounded inner child.

So, if you think back to eighth grade, when people got valentines from their friends but you didn't, and you feel that tug of *ugh* in your stomach? That's your inner child tugging at you, wanting you to reassure them that you are lovable and worthy. You may experience it as heaviness or sadness or maybe a voice saying "No one loved you, even then." (Rude!) That would be the inner critic, but we'll get into their whole deal soon.

Let's use the same example and apply it to the present. Let's say you're out with your friends, and it seems like everyone is talking to each other but not to you. You feel down and may even think, *Why am I always the last one anyone wants to talk to? No one wants to be friends with me.* That would be the wounded inner child part that didn't get those valentines and has coupled not getting those cards in the past with the idea of people not wanting to be its friend *ever.* It may even go further back to rejections from parents that made that time in eighth grade sting even more. So even though on the surface you may judge yourself for overreacting or being "too sensitive," the truth is that the inner child always has a good reason for feeling hurt.

If you are a human on Earth, you have the inner child tugging at you, to varying degrees. There is nothing wrong with it—in fact it's a rich, sensitive, vital part of yourself. You don't even have to have come from trauma to experience the wounded inner child. We all have experienced something that wasn't quite resolved, from something as serious as being othered by systemic racism and homophobia to feeling left out at a sleepover. Comparing pain isn't helpful; it keeps us from healing it. All of our pain deserves our attention.

When an event is not resolved, it can't just disappear. We can't see it with our eyes, but it doesn't dissipate into the ether never to be heard from again. Many times we brush past these feelings or shove them down because they feel like too much or annoying. We are still feeling them, but we are resisting them, hoping that if we just ignore them long enough they will go away. But as Carl Jung said, what we resist persists. And in my experience with feelings, what we resist gets stronger and often comes out sideways.

We've all likely experienced crying over a commercial and thinking, *I have no idea why I'm crying right now!* Or we lashed out at someone and immediately knew that we weren't even mad at that person but didn't know why the anger was just there, ready to explode.

When dealing with feelings, we must meet them head-on for them to truly dissipate. This can be especially annoying to hear for those of us who would much prefer that feelings stay out of things (unless they are happy feelings!). I have heard many a client say something along the lines of "Why can't they just go away? I don't need them!"

But stay they do, until we shine a light on them and hopefully understand them and give them self-compassion. When we do that, we will feel integrated and understood. By directly working with that part of ourselves, the inner child, we are able to come to a resolution not just with that issue in the moment, but also with past hurts. You may be surprised to find that you feel resolution after working with yourself on an issue that has been bothering you, when you thought you'd always need an apology from someone else or other closure from an external source. The more we communicate with our inner child, the more we feel heard and seen, and the more we start to feel safe within ourselves and less plagued by the past.

We heal. We integrate the part of ourselves that has felt pushed aside and dismissed with the rest of us. We give ourselves permission to experience all of ourselves, not just cherry-picked acceptance of various traits we've deemed good enough.

As an intuitive reader and healer, I work with people by looking within their energy fields to see what is underneath the issues they are coming to me with. They are mad at their partner because they brushed them off, but what is the root of that pain? Is it feeling ignored, dismissed, not seen? In almost every session with people I see their inner child, because nine times out of ten, this is where that root pain originated.

That time you got upset with your partner for forgetting to pick up apples on the way home, even though you knew on paper there was nothing to be upset about? That's coming from your inner child. Maybe when you were younger, your parents always forgot to pick you up from school or said they would get you things you wanted but rarely followed through. You grew up and "forgot" about it, but your inner child didn't.

Or maybe the problem that seemed like nothing really *was* something to be upset about: it's not that your partner forgot the apples, but that it's symptomatic of an imbalance in the relationship. But your reaction made it impossible for you to stay centered about that issue in the moment, because the feelings were overwhelming. On those occasions, it is highly likely that the part of yourself that is reacting is rooted in older feelings of hurt or anger. It's rooted in your dad promising he would come to your game and finding excuses at the last minute as to why he couldn't. So yes, sometimes when you feel strongly about something that has happened, you have every right to be upset, but you then have to sort through the delicate balance of what is yours and what is theirs.

Let me reiterate: even if your reaction is rooted in trauma, you still have a right to be upset! All feelings are valid. What's not okay is when we blame other people for those feelings, especially when the pain is coming from an old wound (the inner child) and we attribute the full weight of what we are experiencing to the present argument.

Does it mean you are overreacting? Not at all. If there really is an imbalance in the relationship that needs to be addressed, that is real. But it is also possible that simultaneously it's activating your wounded inner child and part of you needs to know you hear them. Once they feel better after being seen by you, you can better know how to address the situation without being merged with your inner child.

Cindy was a client of mine who grew up without a father after he left her family when she was only five years old. He did not give an explanation and rarely spoke to her after that day. Naturally, she was very hurt from this experience. She didn't have the tools yet to soothe and validate the inner child that still felt his absence acutely. She had a flourishing and fulfilling career, but found herself drawn to relationships where she had to prove herself in order to get love.

She was seeing a man who was intermittent with his communication and had a tendency to give and then withdraw love. So this was a case where both her inner child was activated and her relationship was not giving her the reliability she needed to feel safe. The man was not reliable in a relationship, and it was also hitting her old wound of abandonment.

Through dialoguing with her inner child (which we will learn about soon), Cindy was able to see how she was abandoning *herself.* She saw how when he would pull away, she would pull away from herself as well, trying desperately to figure him out instead of figuring out what *she* needed. She began to build a relationship with her inner loving adult where she showed up for herself more and developed trust within. Through this trust, Cindy also learned by dialoguing with her inner child that she didn't feel safe with her boyfriend.

When her boyfriend didn't return her texts, it brought up all the feelings of being abandoned again from childhood, which were disproportionate to the present situation. But her boyfriend was also not reliable and not someone who could be in the type of relationship she wanted. The question then changes from "Am I overreacting?" to "What unmet need requires my attention right now?" When you understand this dynamic, you can begin to address the core issue and get clear about what is actually happening in the moment.

It can also happen that you are responding to a past pain alone, and the person in front of you is not doing anything to trigger it. My client Marsha was raised with narcissistic parents who were overly concerned with how well she did in school and obsessed with her being thin. Her way of creating safety as a child was to be achievement oriented. She knew if she performed well in school and was thin enough for her parents' standards, they would give her love. She also knew that if she didn't do well, they would withdraw their love. They would criticize her and become cold toward her. This can feel like death to a child. Parental rejection in childhood feels life threatening because we have no way to survive without our parents. It creates a desperation in the child to get their love, and they live in survival mode until they get it.

During one of our sessions Marsha told me about a situation where a friend of hers, whom she idealized, had asked about a shirt she was wearing. Marsha took offense, assuming the friend was pointing out her shirt because it wasn't as expensive as the clothes that this friend wore. However, it was clear, even though I was hearing only Marsha's side of the story, that the friend meant nothing by it and genuinely liked the shirt.

Marsha got very angry with her friend and, after a terse interaction, blocked her from her phone and social media accounts. Through our session we were able to identify that Marsha's inner child felt so threatened by her friend's perceived success that it brought up all of her feelings of inadequacy from childhood. This inadequacy felt like a life-and-death threat, just like it did in childhood.

Marsha was not reacting to what was happening in the moment, but rather to the threat of early childhood survival. After our session, Marsha was able to see the truth of the source of her pain, but unfortunately not everything gets tied up in a neat bow. Her friend set a boundary, and they were not able to repair the friendship.

Still, Marsha was able to notice her reactions in the future and become mindful of the fact that she was often reacting from her wound, which is the first step. When she learned the techniques of dialoguing with her inner child and learning how to soothe that part of herself, she was able to catch herself before she lashed out in the future. As time went on and her inner child felt like Marsha didn't need her to be on a certain level in order to be loved, this kind of thing was rarely a trigger. If it did come up, she was able to address it right away and make herself feel heard and seen.

You may notice I didn't say that it was never a trigger ever again. This is pretty big programming she had to override! I do believe that over time it will be possible for her to completely feel safe and not feel triggered, but growth is not a straight line, and it's unrealistic to think that all this might go away after only a few conversations with her inner child. The relationship with your secure inner adult takes time to build trust, just like any other, and she will feel trusting of herself if she commits to it. When you begin to build this relationship, remember that it will take time for you, too—but you may begin to see results in your interactions with friends and family right away.

Are We *Ever* Overreacting?

In the example I used above, Marsha was overreacting in the way most people use that term. She wasn't reacting in proportion to the situation she was dealing with in the present. She was instead reacting proportionally to the inner child's wound of the past. If I was her friend, I would definitely think of it as an overreaction. It simply was not in the reality of the present moment.

And yet . . . I still caution against using the term *overreacting* when we are examining our behavior. It comes with judgment and even shame, and we cannot grow from that place. Of course we need to be able to judge a situation, but that is different from judging our feelings as being too much or wrong. When instead we reframe our reaction by understanding it with curiosity rather than criticism, we can see where there is room for growth and change.

When we do that, we can unmerge from our inner child and see the reality of the present moment. In Marsha's case, she could then see *Okay, I really was not reacting to what was happening. My friend was just trying to give me a compliment.* Then she could give herself compassion, apologize, and move on.

Throughout this book, we will go into how to start in this place in order to do work with our inner child. Most important, we'll need to establish our loving inner parent first. In the class I teach on working with the inner child, the first module is all about developing the inner parent, because all of this work needs to be grounded from that place before we do anything else.

The inner parent needs to be in the driver's seat. Imagine if you let a six-year-old drive you around. Unless your driver is a very tall six-year-old, they literally won't be able to see where they are going and can't reach the brakes. They'll probably stop a lot for ice cream when you have somewhere else you need to be. And they might look away from the road a lot to yell at their brother. In real life, when your inner six-year-old is at the emotional wheel, it can feel equally jarring. It also explains the lack of impulse control—especially when your brother *is* annoying!

If the inner adult is not in charge, you are merged with the inner child. When this happens, you don't have the neutrality that the inner parent is able to have, which is what you need to feel your most free, authentic self and make the best decisions for your life.

Before we get further into understanding the different aspects of the inner child, I want to say a word about this idea of even having different voices or parts of ourselves that live within us. We appear to each other as being one unified person with one voice inside. And obviously, we do have one literal voice. But how many times have you heard "I'm of two minds about this" or "I am split on how I feel about this." How many people do you know who are behaving in ways you know they don't want to behave? We only need to look at times when we tell ourselves we are going to quit smoking, stop eating a certain way, or change any other habit and then do the opposite. In those situations, it's easy to see that there is definitely more than one part of us operating our psyche.

Historically, the idea of having multiple parts living inside of us has been demonized and looked at as mental illness, which in and of itself has so much stigma attached to it (wrongfully so). And there is a mental illness called dissociative identity disorder where people do in fact split more severely into disparate psychological parts. There is no shame in knowing when you have mental illness and doing what you need to do to take care of yourself. So many people suffer from it needlessly because of the shame around admitting it. But recognizing that your psyche consists of different parts is not necessarily an indicator of mental illness. It just means that you are a human. But because it is so pathologized, sometimes people get scared about delving into the various parts of their personality, thinking that if they do, it's going to prove how unwell they are. The truth is that it is extremely healthy to explore more of who you are and become attuned to the many aspects of yourself. They exist whether you are aware of them or not, and acknowledging them brings them to the light, where you can heal them. The more we know ourselves, and the more we accept all of our thoughts and feelings, the more unified we can become so we can follow through with what we want to do and show up authentically.

When we hold back emotions, they become stronger, until we look at them and accept them. You can't ignore a feeling into oblivion. The same is true for ignoring the parts of ourselves that are trying to be heard. No one goes about their day without feeling conflicting thoughts. But we're much happier when we have a strong, loving inner parent at the helm who accepts them.

The Shadow and the Inner Child

The opposite of bringing your inner child to the light so you can see them and heal them is pushing them down into your shadow where you don't have to deal with them at all. The shadow, which was an idea first conceived of by Carl Jung, is the idea that we all have parts of ourselves that we reject and therefore we send them to the "shadows" of our psyche. When we judge our thoughts and feelings, we send them away into the darkness of our subconscious so we can then live happily ever after! JK—this doesn't work. What actually ends up happening is that these feelings come out sideways. You end up snapping at your partner for putting the dishes away wrong ("Yes, there *is* a right way, *Carol!*"). Except that you don't really care about the dishes; you're mad at your boss, but you feel powerless because you can't tell *her* off. Or, in a bigger example, you don't want to face the pain of the relationship with your father, but you end up attracting that same kind of relationship over and over, which makes you miserable. As Carl Jung said, "Until you make the unconscious conscious, it will rule your life and you will call it fate."

The wounded inner child is part of this shadow. If we are rejecting the inner child's needs, feeling that they are not important or that they are shameful, then you cannot heal them. You cannot heal what you can't see. There is a wealth of information in the feelings of your wounded inner child, and when examined, it can lead you to feeling happier, more satisfied, and complete. Inner child healing, then, is a form of shadow work.

Think about your closest relationships. If you come home and find your partner quietly brooding about something without telling you why they're upset, or if they are lashing out at you without explaining their actions, that is the not fun combination of poor communication and hurt feelings. Until you address this dynamic, you might feel angry or anxious. The same thing happens with ourselves when we shut down communication with the parts of us that are feeling upset. Then we might end up feeling grumpy all day without understanding why or checking out by binge watching or mindless eating.

The most important relationship we have is with ourselves. This relationship affects everything in our lives. It's the center point from which everything else flows. So why wouldn't we want to have fulfilling communication with all of the parts of ourselves, including the inner child?

Just like in any relationship, if you open up communication with your inner child, you will have a much more enriching and satisfying connection. Remember: you have a fun, playful, creative part of you that is the inner child. They are not wounded, and they are still very much a part of you. That side of you comes out more and more the more you feel seen and heard. That is such an important part of why we are here: to do the things that bring us joy and add light to the world, and to bring those qualities to other people.

So how can you even know if your inner child needs your attention? Maybe it's obvious to you, but in case it isn't, here are some ways to know that your wounded inner child is asking for attention:

- You are in any situation where you are feeling your feelings but you feel a lack of internal support.

- You feel lonely.

- You're indulging in things you know you don't want to. This is sometimes called lack of willpower.

- You're procrastinating.

- You are obsessing.

- You're feeling guilty or responsible.

- You're doubting yourself.

- You minimize your feelings.

- You are stuck in a feeling of lack, like there are no options or only limited resources.

- You are thinking in extremes or black-and-white terms.

These are just some indicators that your inner child could benefit from more connection with your inner adult.

But I'm Scared!! What If I Can Never Close This Can of Emotional Worms?

First of all, I'm so sorry I called them emotional worms, because that is a ridiculous thing to say. And second of all, this is a very natural and also common concern. You absolutely need to go at a pace that feels safe and doable for you. I don't want anyone diving into emotions when they don't feel they are in a place to handle it.

That said, there is *only* good that will come from building your connection to your inner adult. In fact, that fear of not being able to handle it is an indication that you are merged with the inner child and not feeling connected to a loving internal parent.

So if you feel like there is no way you are messing with that kid in the basement right now, I totally get it. But let's get to know the adult in charge, so you can build a strong connection with the part of you that *is* able to handle it. And I promise you, you do have that part of yourself.

Spoiler alert: it is highly likely that what you fear the inner child might have to say is much worse than what it actually is. I have never seen anyone who, talking from their inner adult, felt anything but softness, relief, connection, and joy—just to name a few beneficial feelings—after making contact with their inner child. Yes, there have also been times when it was hard to stay centered in the adult, and that felt overwhelming because they were merging with all of the emotions of the child. But that's why I advise that you get centered in the adult before you begin to get to know your inner child. Then, when you're ready, remember to progress as slowly as you need to.

If you like, continue on to the chapter on energy healing, which will help you build up the inner adult, or feel free to skip ahead and read the inner adult chapter before you do the following exercises. Or read through it all and see how you feel. But above all, you know what's best for you—validate that.

Practice Getting to Know Your Inner Child

The following practices and meditation will help you begin getting to know your inner child. I want to reassure you that gaining progress doesn't have to be a years-long process. In fact, any time you connect, even for a moment, you are changing the pathways in your brain to become more ready to support and honor yourself. Every time you connect, you will experience a deeper sense of self and resilience.

But even though the process of getting to know the inner child doesn't need to be a lifelong inquiry, what you will gain is a lifelong relationship. Just like you can never know everything about the person you are closest to, you can never know everything there is to know about yourself. You will be getting to know yourself throughout your whole life. But if you start this process, before too long you will know when you have taken on other people's energy, when you have crossed your own boundary, what is yours or someone else's, when you need to say no, what your intuition is telling you, and so much more.

Observing Your Inner Child

Start to acknowledge your reactive feelings for what they are: your inner child. *Reactive* is not a judgmental term. We all react to things all day long—that is part of being a human. It's a good sign that you're not a robot! In this exercise, we are breaking down the source of these reactions and figuring out where they are coming from so that we can attune to them and integrate them. In the next chapters we will get into the inner loving parent, where we will delve further into how to lovingly interact. But for now, a good start is simply putting your hand on your heart while you notice your inner child. Simply notice.

Here's an example: You're scrolling on social media and start to notice that you are getting upset. Or you finish scrolling and you notice that you are feeling drained. Put your hand on your heart and simply tune in to how you are feeling. Where are you feeling it in your body? Are you feeling down about yourself? What feelings come up? Just recognize these thoughts and emotions as not being "you"—as in the totality of who you are, your true self—but your inner child.

If the feelings you notice are not really feelings at all but in fact criticisms, notice that too as being your inner critic. That's it! Just notice.

Another example: You get into an argument with your partner. They leave to clear their mind, and you feel a lot of feelings. Maybe those are anger or sadness. Once again, put your hand on your heart and, from that place, notice how you are feeling. You may even want to look down as if your inner child is in your lap, to get a sense that you are looking at the feelings (the inner child) as opposed to *being* the feelings. I also love imagining that my inner child is in my lap or sitting next to me. These are all ways of getting separation in your awareness and untangling your inner adult from the complicated web of feelings and thoughts you may be processing.

We're starting simply here. There's no need to dive into the emotional aspect of what is happening—we're simply bringing awareness in so you can begin to learn where the inner child lives and recognize it.

Meditation

Meditation can be very helpful in terms of changing the neural pathways in your brain, replacing old habits and patterns with ones that support you. Your subconscious mind doesn't know the difference between what really happened and what you are visualizing you wish had happened. When you are in meditation, your brain becomes more able to receive the information and programming you are giving it. This in turn helps you to reprogram old reactions that aren't serving you. For instance, if your subconscious can start to believe that you feel deeply loved because you have visualized that in meditation, you will feel more deeply loved in your awakened state. The following meditation will help you do that.

Reprogramming a Childhood Experience

1. Get into a comfortable position and close your eyes.

2. Take a deep breath and scan your body, starting with your head and moving down to your feet.

3. Simply notice any place where you are holding tension.

4. Don't do anything with that tension; just notice it. Take a breath and observe as your body naturally releases anything it's holding.

5. Find yourself floating up to a large sun above your head.

6. Now call in gold light, allowing it to fill your body.

7. Let yourself bask in that light.

8. Feel yourself surrounded by a loving presence. You know this presence is there to shine more and more love into you and protect you.

9. Feel the loving presence around you guide you to see what is in front of you.

10. Notice a timeline. It may look like train tracks, or maybe it is just a line—however it displays itself to you is fine. Notice it light up in a certain area indicating the past.

11. Go to that part of the timeline.

12. See yourself as a young child at a time that was very challenging for you.

13. Take a deep breath, and when you are ready, watch the event—or if it's too much, just know you are there.

14. Now imagine the event going as you wished it would.

15. See the whole situation happen as if it occurred in the most loving, peaceful way.

16. You can add people who weren't there. You can make up totally new circumstances. Do whatever you need to do to make yourself feel completely loved or however you needed to feel in that moment.

17. When you are ready, feel yourself supported by your guide, leading you back to the sun.

18. Find yourself back at the sun, immersed in the light.

19. Float back down into your body.

20. When you are ready, wiggle your fingers and toes and gently come back into the room.

CHAPTER TWO

Energy Healing

E nergy healing is often perceived as being too "woo," or out there, or something for the special few. The truth is that none of these perceptions are true. Energy healing is something anyone can benefit from, and it is extremely beneficial for inner child healing. After all, our inner child is a part of our energy field.

Our energy field is made up of unseen matter that is at a higher vibration than our physical body. Our physical body is just one means by which we interact with the world, but because it is the one that we can sense with our five senses, it's the one that people are most familiar with. It's also the one that people rely on to interact with the world and care for them-selves. When we start to take care of our energy body as well as our physical body, that unseen part of ourselves feels more tangible even if we can't see it (although some people can). Like the physical body, your energy body has many parts, and it is where your feelings, spirit, patterns of behavior, the inner child, and other aspects are stored.

When I began learning energy healing more than twenty years ago, I was in a marriage that didn't excite either me or my husband, a very nice, stable guy. I had convinced myself that the relationship was as good as anyone could have, not only because—but definitely a lot because—everyone around me told me how great he was and how great he was for *me*.

And he *was* great! There was nothing wrong with him—and a lot right!

But after not too long, I realized I was no longer in love with him.

I had a tendency to be flighty in relationships, I told myself. (This wasn't actually true.) I had rom-com hopes for a relationship! (That actually *was* true and part of the problem.) I felt that the way to get a rom-com-worthy life was to settle in with this very nice person who everyone agreed was very good for me.

The night we got engaged, I sobbed the entire night—and I'm not a crier. I had no idea why I was crying. I was happy! *Ish?*

About a year into our marriage I began to learn the form of energy healing that I practice, which, to simplify it, is based on the idea that the clearer your energy is, the more you can know yourself. As I started to clear out my energy, I started hearing my own inner voice speaking the truth of what I wanted and needed louder and louder. I started being able to separate the beliefs about myself that my parents had handed down to me from my own beliefs about myself and who I was. I began to get clear about what I really wanted. I started to feel more present and less in my head. I started to know the difference between what it felt like to get other people's information and how it felt to get my own.

I started to understand why I couldn't stop crying the night I got engaged. My inner voice was screaming at me: *This isn't right!* And my inner child felt sad and hopeless that I was giving over the power of this decision to other people in my life rather than listening to her. The clearer my energy field was, the more it became clear that I had abandoned myself the night I accepted the engagement.

Energy healing and inner child healing are so linked because our feelings live in our energy field as well as in our physical body. When we work with one, we are working with the other.

I decided to leave my first husband, and literally everyone thought I was making the worst possible decision. They told me I was crazy. They thought my ex-husband grounded me, keeping me "sane" while I lived my free-spirited life.

They didn't know that I was capable of providing that grounding for myself.

To be honest, I didn't either. I was freaking terrified to leave. He was nice! He was safe, and our relationship was easy!

We were good friends! He also had money and a stable job, and we were living in New York City, so my fears of financial instability became very loud.

But once I heard my inner voice speaking louder than the one that told me what I "should" do, I didn't want to look back. When I listened to what I wanted, my life felt expansive and exciting while also being grounded. I was terrified *and* happier than I'd ever been.

It was the best decision I've ever made. And this is not to insult my ex-husband at all. He's a nice guy who is now happily married; we were just not a great fit for a long-term relationship.

Not long after my first husband and I officially separated, I met my husband of now eighteen years, and guess what? I'm still in love with him!

You may wonder, what does energy healing have to do with any of this?

The practice of the kind of energy healing I do—there are many different styles—involves becoming aware of your energetic system and energetic boundaries. When I was unaware of them, I was far less in touch with who I was in general, and often couldn't discern between what I wanted, felt, and needed and what other people did. This isn't the case for everyone, but it often is the case for many who had their experiences invalidated while they were growing up. That is just one reason why this may happen, but the truth is that there are innumerable reasons why we check out and disengage from our own true feelings.

Because of my history, I leaned toward codependency. My experiences as a child taught me that I was worthy only if I was taking care of my mother's feelings. This wasn't said explicitly, but it showed up in ways you may (or may not) recognize in your own life. For me it looked like this:

- **My mother would get angry if I said I needed something that went against what she wanted.**

- **She was competitive with me, viewing me as her adversary. If I had a success, she would withdraw, but if I didn't succeed, she would criticize me.**

- **If I expressed being upset with her, she would get angry and leave or coolly reject me instead of hearing me out.**

- **I felt very loved when she was the focus, shining her light on me, making me feel like I was doing a good job.**

- **If I didn't do well in school or a performance of any kind, I was either outright made to feel like I was bad, or she would withdraw emotionally and get cold.**

- **She would give me things and then criticize me for how well or not well I took care of them.**

My father also had a role in this, but his job took him away most of the time and he was much more accepting of me in general. However, as an adult, I saw that he too could only tolerate my being a certain way; it just so happened that that was the way I had been naturally, most of my life.

I bring all of this up because it affected how I held my energy and where I gave my power. (Away, mostly.) Because I was trained in the fine art of codependency, my energy would automatically go out to everyone around me, gradually but steadily being depleted. I would take responsibility for what wasn't mine—even though, many times no one was asking me to do that—and I often became unclear about what I was feeling as opposed to what other people were feeling. I was so used to taking on other people's energies and feeling responsible for their feelings that I usually didn't even know I was doing it. My energy field became a mishmash of mine and other people's. I would walk into a room and suddenly feel great or terrible depending on who was in there, because unbeknownst to me, my aura had a flashing "Open 24/7" sign on it. It was *wide* open and vulnerable to anyone around me.

When your energy is open like this, it goes out indiscriminately. This means you will often pick up on other people's feelings. Why not, after all, when you were taught that this behavior is "nice" and that boundaries are selfish? Why not prioritize others' needs when you were abandoned for asserting your own as a child? And when you are rewarded for taking on the emotional burdens of the people around you, you will keep doing it. In fact, that is how you feel safe. You may not enjoy it, but you have been wired to believe that taking care of others is the best way to gain safety and acceptance, and steering off that path is the road to rejection.

The word *empath* is thrown out a lot these days, and picking up on feelings like this is a sign of an empath. What we often aren't told is that this trait is often (but not always) a result of trauma experienced while growing up. When children have to be aware of what everyone is feeling or not be safe, they will likely develop the superpower of empathy. Growing up this can look like:

- Being able to tell when your alcoholic father is in a bad mood and knowing just what he needs to keep him in check.

- Sensing when your mother, who suffers from depression, is about to sink back into it.

- Feeling what everyone in your house is going through when they are arguing.

- Feeling deeply when you have disappointed your parent, even if that disappointment is not reasonable.

Translated into adult life, this "superpower" can look like:

- Thinking you know how everyone is feeling, even though they haven't told you. (Maybe

you're right, but it's not kind or respectful
to assume!)

- Feeling drained because you are taking care
  of everyone around you.

- Jumping in to be the mediator when friends
  or family are fighting.

- Feeling like everything is your
  responsibility and becoming exhausted and
  depleted because of it.

When you learn how to simply be aware of your energy, you start to bring your power back. One of the first things I learned with energy healing was what my aura was. I began to understand how I could feel it and know if it was with someone else or if it was centered around me. This tool alone helped me to feel more clear and centered, so I'll start there.

Have you ever had the experience of feeling someone looking at you, or coming up behind you, but you didn't see them do that with your eyes? That is the experience of feeling someone's energy.

Your aura is the bubble of energy around your physical body. When you are picking up on other people in this way, you are feeling them with your aura, or what some people call the subtle energy body. When you have codependency traits, like wanting to take responsibility for others, your aura will naturally spread out into other people's, like mine did. When you become aware of how to be in touch with yours, you can sense right away when you are doing that and bring your energy back.

Codependency isn't the only reason our energy goes out. Sometimes it may be because we want to control a situation (understandably, because it's hard to be a human without control), or we are overexerting ourselves and are exhausted. There are many reasons, and being aware of your aura can help you feel fortified, able to let go of the need for control, and more centered. This method of accessing your own strength and stability can be incredibly practical and useful in your day-to-day life.

The overexpansion of your aura isn't the only way psychological dysfunction can affect your energy fields. If you have strong inner child protectors (another way of saying that you feel guarded and protective of your energy), your aura may be contracted and tight around your space. If this is the case, you can feel shut down in your chakras as well (we'll get to that subject in a minute). If your aura is contracted, it can look like:

- **Feeling perfectionistic toward yourself.**

- **Having a hard time expressing yourself.**

- **Feeling rigid.**

- **Having a strong need to control situations and your emotions.**

- **Having a hard time accepting viewpoints other than your own.**

- **Having a hard time letting people in.**

- **Being judgmental of your own (and sometimes others') vulnerability.**

The first step in working with your aura is simply starting to be aware of it. Once you're aware of it, then you can know how it feels when you're feeling good and when you're feeling constricted or drained (or anything in between).

Mindfulness is one of many superpowers we have. If we aren't aware, we can't adjust to make the changes we want in our life. Many of the tools we use in energy healing are so subtle that it would be easy to dismiss them as not being powerful. But subtle does not equal minimal—in fact, energy healing techniques are hugely efficient and helpful. In our very masculine-dominated world, we are trained to think that big, flashy ways of doing things are the best ways to get results. We're often encouraged to make changes like pushing past our mental blocks using willpower, cutting toxic people out of our lives, or saying yes to things we're scared of. Those actions can be very powerful, but they are not the only way to improve ourselves. They are simply more obvious. Mindfulness, self-compassion, and techniques to adjust our energy are all equally powerful, and in some cases they're a better way to make lasting changes.

So first, be aware of that sense when you know someone is there but they haven't said anything yet. That's you being aware of at least part of your aura. See if you can extend that awareness to your entire aura, which is like an egg shape around your body. Don't forget to mentally search the area above and below you. One trick I learned is to rub your hands together, creating friction. Then, with your palms hovering about two feet away from your body, see if you can feel the subtle energy. If you have a hard time with that, try it with a friend. See if it's easier to feel their energy.

Even if you don't have it down yet, don't worry. The art of learning the language of your energy field involves a lot of trust. For those of us who were taught to distrust our information, even the very beginning of learning this can be a challenge. Just know you are not alone. When people take my energy healing class, the number one thing they need reassurance about is that they can take the leap and trust that what they're seeing or feeling is real.

A quick caveat to that: when you are in the process of doing an exercise like this, definitely trust yourself! Just like when you're watching a movie and you suspend your disbelief, when you're doing the exercise, implement that. Once you're out of it, you can bring in the analyzer part of yourself and ask, *Okay, did that feel real? Could that be true?* Sometimes we all get information that feels "off." There are many reasons for that, anything from not being centered or grounded to guides that pop in to give their perspective without you realizing it. You will make mistakes. But you won't ever know what's true and what isn't if you doubt yourself the entire time.

Let's say that you are now aware of your aura to at least some degree. Think of someone you love and feel safe with—it can be a pet or a plant if you can't think of a person. (I'm certain that the more you do inner child healing and energy healing, the more you will discover supportive people in your life.) Now imagine your aura going out to meet this person. Imagine your aura spreading out over to them, as if you were standing next to them. It should be near them, but not invading their space—that's important.

Now imagine your aura coming back to you. Can you sense the difference between how it felt when your aura was centered on you, as opposed to divided between you and someone or something else? Try this exercise again with a different person. Don't try to do it with someone who is too challenging or someone who doesn't have the best boundaries with you. Pick someone with whom you have a positive or neutral relationship. See what it feels like to spread your energy over to them. Then call it back. What do you notice?

You may find that you feel feelings that you didn't expect, or that you feel more powerful now that you have a better command of your energy. Hopefully this little exercise showed you what it feels like when you have control of your aura and what it feels like when it is firmly centered on you.

This practice of stretching your aura is strictly for the exercise of understanding how it feels when you are spread too

A Quick Note about Spirit Guides

I'm going to assume you believe in spirit guides or are at least open to the possibility that they are real. We always have the choice to have power over our energetic space, and if we're feeling we're giving it away, we can consciously claim it. Sometimes people are eager to connect to their spirit guides because they think they have all the answers. The truth is that guides are a lot like people: there are helpful ones and unhelpful ones. The helpful ones have good boundaries, just like people. They will not get in your energetic field. When you ask to communicate with them, they respond without crossing the boundary of your aura. When we allow random guides to come into our space, it can make us cloudy and unsure about what information is ours and what is theirs. It's very similar to when people cross our boundaries; we can become confused and feel unclear about what we need and want if we don't hold steady to our truth.

When I communicate with guides, I always ask to speak only to my highest possible guides, which protects my boundaries. But if you feel like there might be a guide in your space, all you have to do to reclaim it is to have the intention to do so. Ask anything that doesn't serve your higher good to leave. You don't even have to feel it happening—you just have to ask. That's how much power we have over our space. It's helpful afterward to breathe in golden light to fill the space left behind.

Two things can get in the way of claiming your energy field: fear and responsibility. If it's fear, we just need to get back to neutrality by remembering that no one can get in if we don't allow it and that we have a right to our space. It's really that simple, but it doesn't mean it's easy. It can be, but it can also definitely be challenging. This is true with both people and spirits, but it's easier with spirits because most of the time they won't put up a fight.

When clients who come to me have guides in their space, I simply ask them to leave without any fear, because I'm not afraid. I have found that my respect for them combined with the lack of permission for them to come into my space allows them to leave. I understand that this can be different for different people, especially if they are new to it or if the energy is especially intense. But so far, every time I have kept up my neutrality, we have all left the experience on good terms.

The other part is the responsibility piece. We can give our power away if we feel like we don't have a right to say no. But developing a relationship with your spirit guides is a great practice because it is so easy to ask them to leave if they're no longer serving you. All you have to do is ask. With people, it can get stickier, because our real-world issues with them can make us feel responsible for their emotions and happiness. But if you want people to leave you alone in real life, of course you have every right to set that boundary.

thin. I do not recommend sending your energy to other people on purpose. Notice that I suggested spreading it to them but not entering their energy field, and again, that was just for this exercise. As a rule, if we are in people's space, they have to agree on some level. Agreement from them could be anything from enjoying having you there to wanting to control you because they are mad. The same goes for us. In general, it's not a good idea to get up inside someone's energetic grill (so to speak).

If you have been keeping your aura close, how did it feel to extend it far away from you? Was it scary? Did you feel protective, like you didn't trust other people enough to have your aura extended toward them? Whatever came up for you is simply information for you to be aware of. You can also try, the next time you do this exercise, to extend your aura a little more than you did the last time, pushing yourself out of your comfort zone to see what comes up for you then.

Whichever version you experienced, the next time you are feeling drained—maybe while you're at a party or in a Zoom meeting—call your energy back to you. If it's an especially challenging situation, do it multiple times. If you're feeling shut down, see how it feels to make your aura a bit larger.

When you are done with the exercise, breathe in the light. You may want to picture a big sun above your head. Imagine poking a hole in it and feel or sense the light pouring through your body and aura. Then feel, sense, or see it going all the way down your feet and into the earth.

Light is a powerful tool for energy healing and feeling clearer. It's my go-to tool for clearing out energy. The most common comment I hear from clients who come to me for energy healing is that they feel lighter after I work with them. I know the reason they feel this way is because we have cleared out a bunch of stuck energy and they have replaced it with light.

You do not have to feel the light coming into your energy field or even need to feel the effects of it for it to work. Just like when you take a vitamin, you may not feel the effect, but it's still doing its job. It's the same with light. After you call your energy back to you, simply have the intention to breathe in light.

When I was in the process of leaving my first husband, one of the old habits that came up for me strongly was self-doubt. I didn't realize this at the time, but self-doubt can be habitual, and so can obsessing, criticizing yourself, judging others, making yourself small, and other self-limiting patterns. We could call this a default neuropathway that your brain is used to traveling down as you move out of a comfort zone. Taking this well-traveled road was something that was likely reinforced in your childhood when you were seeking connection or expressing yourself.

During this time, I was stepping into my power in a very proactive way, and that brought up all of my old programming around self-worth, which in turn brought out the self-doubt. Who was I to do something that everyone around me told me was a bad idea? Why should I trust, of all people, *myself*? I was raised to keep a firm eye on what my mother wanted—or else. To do the opposite of that was to risk abandonment and disdain.

My environment as an adult was much more supportive than it had been when I was growing up. But that didn't mean that my inner child didn't feel all of those abandonment feelings as if it could be happening now.

My mother actually did stop talking to me for six months when I told her I was getting divorced, so some of my self-doubt was getting validated in the present. But what wasn't true was that her abandonment of me at thirty-one would affect my life the same way it did when I was a child. Still, the programming and habits came up as I initiated a major change in my life.

Another powerful way to think about our energy is how we feel grounded or centered in it. Grounding, energetically speaking, is crucial for us when we are making big changes in our life. Grounding in this case means being connected to your body instead of spacey and disconnected from yourself and others, and being in the present as opposed to ruminating in your mind about the past or present.

To me, being grounded means being able to experience my emotions without checking out emotionally and knowing that I can handle whatever is coming up. When I think of people who are grounded, I think of people who can stay calm in the midst of stress. Celebrities that come to mind are Mr. Rogers, Michelle Obama, Oprah, and Michael Landon from *Little House on the*

Prairie: they project a calm, secure energy. Think of people in your life whom you feel secure around. Now tune in to your body—how does that feel? That is the feeling of being grounded.

We all have a grounding cord, which is an energy cord that hooks into your first chakra at the base of your spine and connects to the middle of the earth. It brings your spirit fully into your body and connects you to the nurturing, present-time energy of the earth.

The first chakra is associated with safety, survival, and security. So you can imagine that when we are doing something really scary—like shaking up our entire lives, for instance—and we aren't connected to our first chakra, it will feel *very* destabilizing.

Not being connected in this way can look like:

- **Feeling spacey.**

- **Feeling scared about the future.**

- **Feeling lost in lack mentality or being sure that there will never be enough.**

- **Feeling codependent, the need to rely on others for our safety.**

- **Being confused or disconnected from our sense of stability.**

When I learned about grounding myself energetically, it changed my life. I was more able to hear my intuition, and I felt surer that I could trust what I was feeling. I stopped losing things and feeling spacey, and I felt present consistently for maybe the first time in my life. I also felt more strongly that I could provide security for myself.

The great thing is that grounding yourself is pretty easy to do. You can start by being in touch with your grounding cord. You can imagine it like a simple cord, a tree trunk, or even a garbage chute—anything that connects to the earth. Then you can imagine any energy or feeling that you are ready to let go of go down the cord into the earth, where it will naturally get recycled. When you sense or see the cord there, affirm that it is in present time, in the geographical location that you are in now. You can then bring in light to help do a further clearing and replace the unwanted energy with your highest information.

Another great energy healing tool is thinking about someone you admire who is firmly grounded and imagining what that sense of grounding feels like. Imagine what that feels like in your own body, and then amplify that feeling. *Anything you admire in someone else also exists in you.* That's why you resonate with it.

The next time you are feeling anxious, think about someone you feel grounded and secure around. Imagine that they are hugging you or you're sitting near them. Bring that sensation of how you feel with them into your body. When you have a good sense of that, use your thumb and forefinger to squeeze the place between your opposite hand's thumb and forefinger. (That's a Neuro-Linguistic Programming trick that I have found very useful.)

Another way to ground is to sit down with your feet on the floor. Your feet have chakras (energy centers) too, and bringing up energy from the earth into them is a fast way to feel connected to the grounding energy of the earth. You know the feeling when you are out in nature and everything feels peaceful? To me, that's the energy of the earth. Without the noise of the city, we're able to really take it in and feel it. Now imagine breathing that energy in through your feet and up your legs. This earth energy that you are consciously taking in brings in the grounding of the present moment.

It feels so magical when you start to notice how using these tools affects your life in such practical and sustaining ways.

Chakra Energy

Chakras are centers in our energy body. The concept of chakras originated in India and is laid out in a text called the Vedas. The word chakra is Sanskrit for "wheel"—many people see the chakras as a spinning wheel of energy. There are seven main chakras, and each holds vital information about our emotional and spiritual lives. When I work with clients, I look at their chakras to see which one is activated when they are talking about what is coming up for them. I will see pictures, past lives, and other historical information emanating from a different chakra, depending on what is going on for them.

The seven primary chakras are the:

- First or root chakra, which is about survival.

- Second or sacral chakra, which is about sexuality/creativity.

- Third or solar plexus chakra, which is about personal power.

- Fourth or heart chakra, which is about affinity for ourselves and others.

- Fifth or throat chakra, which is about expression.

- Sixth or ajna center, which is about inner knowing and sixth sense.

- Seventh or crown chakra, which is about higher knowing.

If you get quiet and start to tune in to your different chakras, you can start to get a sense of where you are holding outdated information and patterns that no longer serve you. Often, I will see the inner child in the second and third chakras. They are often in the sacral chakra because this is also the center of creativity and playfulness. Even if the inner child is wounded, it can be hiding out there. Sometimes I will also see them in the heart chakra, but I can also see them in the third chakra because this is the center of will and personal power. When we get into power struggles, this chakra will hold that information, and unfortunately sometimes the inner child is a part of this and gets stuck there.

This is obviously a very tiny explanation about an enormous topic, but a chapter on energy healing would not be complete without it!

There are so many more ways energy healing has helped me to feel clearer and more grounded and expansive. I've offered you an introduction to some practices that could help with inner child healing, but I encourage you to pursue additional knowledge about energy healing if it resonates with you.

CHAPTER THREE

Your Inner Parent

I f you are like many people I work with, you didn't have a blueprint for a nurturing, supportive, unconditionally loving parent. Or maybe of two caregivers, you had one who was loving and one who was not. Or maybe you did have a loving parent, but they didn't know how to treat themself kindly or had poor boundaries themself. Whatever the reason, you may struggle with knowing how to be consistently nurturing and kind to yourself.

When I teach my class on inner child healing, I start by focusing on how to increase the role of the inner parent. This is because we need the inner parent to be the loudest voice in our head whenever possible. I have never met someone who had this voice to depend on 24/7, 365 days of the year, but it is very possible for it to be the most frequent voice you hear, the one that guides you through your life. When this is the case, you have a solid base of grounding, validation, and centeredness that enables you to show up for yourself in a consistent way, especially when your inner child feels all the feels. This does not mean that calm, secure presence is there to negate what you are feeling—a true inner parent will never exist so that you can shove those feelings down and ignore them in favor of something that sounds more positive. The inner parent is there to hold space for those feelings so they can do what feelings need to do: move. Or it is there to redirect the mind to the body as a reminder to center on being in the present when you begin to dwell on something negative.

In Internal Family Systems, a therapeutic modality that includes inner child work, practitioners use the 8 C's to describe the qualities you inhabit when you're in the self—which is a term I equate with the inner parent. These qualities are calm, connection, compassion, creativity, clarity, curiosity, confidence, and courage. These are qualities that are dominant when our inner parent is "online."

It can be challenging to stay in that secure place when we view our problems as coming from one singular voice. But when we understand we have a hurt child *part*, as opposed to our entire being feeling hurt, then it gives us the opportunity to view that pain as being a part of ourselves, but not who we *are*.

When my client Susie was growing up, her mother was often in a state of hyperreactivity. Her reactions were often extreme, and she reacted to my client in heightened states of many different emotions much of the time, regardless of what was actually happening. Susie spoke of a time when she was upset about a low grade she had gotten in school. When she talked about it with her mother, her mother got as upset as she was, reacting as if it had happened to her, and offered no solutions. In fact, because Susie's mother was so panicked, she only provided examples of the worst possible future scenarios, making Susie even more upset. This was just one example of many where her mother's nervous system was so out of control that it made it impossible for Susie to calm her own. And just as important, her mother had modeled that becoming immersed in anxiety was how to respond to stressful events. Susie was never shown tools to calm herself, so this stress response followed her into adulthood.

Remember when I spoke earlier about how self-doubt can become a default? This is an example of how hyperreactivity and anxiety can become your reflexive place of existence.

Up until we started working together, when Susie had a stressful experience, her go-to reaction was to become highly anxious and consider the worst possible outcomes. This was totally natural for her, because her subconscious had been programmed in childhood to be hypervigilant. She instinctively and unconsciously believed that this is how she could protect herself.

For Susie, developing the inner loving adult started with observing her habit of going into high alert and inadvertently creating more stress. By observing her own behavior, she gave herself the space to try out the somatic tools I suggested to calm her nervous system. We will go into some of those tools later, but this example illustrates the importance of being aware of how you are experiencing stress in the *body*. You can't fix this kind of anxiety on an intellectual level alone.

We cannot parent ourselves if we are completely enveloped in triggered states of emotions. As the example above shows, when we are young, we need our parents to *not* be reactive when we are having everyday stresses. We need them to be able to see our situations from a larger perspective than we can see them from ourselves, so we can be soothed and seen. That is part of the job of the parent. I'm not saying parents have to be perfect and never react. But when they are consistently reactive, it becomes a problem.

Unfortunately, this was the case for Susie. If she was even five minutes late, she never knew what reaction she would be met with. I am saying this not to villainize her mother but to show one example of what it looks like when we are raised by people who can't soothe themselves or their children because they are enveloped by their own emotion. It makes it hard for the children to grow up and be in anything other than a reactive state with themselves when under stress. It also makes them hypervigilant, always preparing for the next stressful event so they won't be caught off guard. This kind of preparation only serves to keep their inner child insecure, dreaming up the next possible attack.

When we grow up like this or have experienced continued trauma of any kind, as adults we often merge with and behave as the wounded inner child until we can learn that we have someone internally in charge who can care for us: the inner adult.

Susie's mother could not handle her daughter's problems from a neutral perspective because she was merging with her own inner child's state of fear. She could not assess a situation and see the bigger picture, because she was often so off-center (very much not in the 8 C's) that she was seeing only catastrophic possibilities.

How could Susie be expected to then soothe herself or access a state of calm? She had to learn how to do it through tools like inner child healing, because she was taught the opposite as a child. If this is you, I want you to know it is not your fault. Every single human on Earth reverts to the programming that we got as children unless we consciously reprogram ourselves. There are many ways to do this, and even the simple act of becoming mindful is one way to adopt new neural pathways so that you can disrupt that conditioning.

The mother in this case also is not at fault for how she reacts, but she is responsible for how she behaves. Once you become a parent and are responsible for the development of another human's psyche, it is your responsibility to care for yourself so that you don't consciously or unconsciously offload your issues onto someone else. In the case of my client Susie, it's not her fault that she didn't learn to soothe herself, but it is her responsibility to learn how to do that now, so that she doesn't treat herself as the victim in relationships.

Think about a time when you saw a loved one go through something challenging and got caught up in their experience. Maybe you felt like it was almost happening to you, or you wanted to save them. You identified so much with them that you weren't able to be centered and offer real help because you were as caught up in the emotion as they were.

As I talked about in the last chapter, many empaths merge with the emotions of the people around them and end up not being able to be as helpful as they could have if they were able to remain grounded and witness their loved one's issues from a centered place. When we are centered and calm, we can decide if there is a way to help from that place—not from a place of reactivity and panic.

Another situation many of us have experienced is when a friend or someone close to us makes *our* issues about them. When I was going through the divorce from my first husband, my mother became distraught and angry, as if I were doing something to hurt her personally. I said to her, "This is *my* divorce. I'm not doing this *to* you." And she said, "Aren't I allowed to have a reaction?! It's my divorce too!"

Of course she was allowed to have a reaction, but it wasn't actually her divorce. Also, because of her narcissism (and her lack of perspective, which means she wasn't treating it—which is an important distinction, as there are people who have narcissistic personality disorder and are working on themselves

51

to heal it), she could not see how it was more important to consider her daughter's feelings than her own.

This is a somewhat extreme example, but whether we are overcome with empathy or rage, we become unhelpful when we merge with our feelings (our inner children) with problems that aren't actually our own.

When you are situated in the embodiment of the inner parent, you can stop identifying with or *as* the charged emotions you are experiencing. Embodying the inner parent means getting the "bigger picture" feeling that we might have gotten from a trusted adult when we were kids. One of the most satisfying and heartwarming feelings is being able to comfort our inner child and feel an immediate change from challenging feelings like being insecure or upset to feeling confident and soothed.

You know that feeling when you were in school and someone hurt your feelings, and then maybe a parent or teacher said just the right thing to put everything in perspective and make you realize that it was okay? That *you* were okay? That's the feeling you can give your inner child: that you have a secure sense of the bigger picture and that you are there to take care of them. They don't have to do all the work—which is good, because they can't!

We will get into how we can develop the inner adult in the next chapter, but first we'll start by answering the question of how we even know when our loving inner parent isn't around. It may seem like an obvious thing to notice, but it can show up in subtle ways.

Signs Your Loving Inner Parent Is AWOL

- You have difficulty encouraging yourself.

- You have a hard time saying no to other people's needs; boundaries are hard for you.

- You doubt your inner voice.

- When an issue comes up, you can spend time obsessing about it. It's hard to find a supportive way to help yourself out of it.

- You get lost in your anger, sadness, or worry.

- You often feel responsible for other people's feelings.

- You feel like you can't access your intuition.

- You lose time getting mad at yourself over past mistakes.

- You feel like you just are bad, unworthy, or not good enough, either in relation to a situation or in general.

- You are judging who you are in totality based on a situation.

The list above details just a few clues that can tell you that your inner child or inner critic is in charge and that you're seeing the events unfolding in your life through their perspective.

A missing inner parent can manifest in so many other ways. For example, take a moment if you find yourself directionless or doing things that you don't want to be doing. If you find yourself binge-watching TV for hours when you have other things you need to be doing (although there's nothing wrong with a binge-watch in general), if you find yourself mindlessly eating out of boredom, or if you realize you're saying yes to things you wish you had said no to, these are behaviors that can clue you in to the fact that the inner child is in charge.

In these situations, much like a kid who hasn't been given rules, the inner child is acting on impulse. Without having a parent step in to help them do something that will ultimately feel more satisfying, they're probably going to keep scrolling through their phone or watching reruns of *Grey's Anatomy* instead of tuning into what they really need in that moment.

When I get caught up in any of this, I have what I call my "mom globes" on over my eyes. In a meditation, I once saw I had energetic globes over my eyes that limited the ways I perceived myself and other people. I could see that these globes contained all of the programming and energy I had received from my mother. Taking the mom globes off is a way to honor myself and become connected to my true self.

One very important task of the inner parent is to allow whatever feelings are coming up to flow and have their necessary time, while not feeling like we've merged with those feelings or identifying *as* them. It's so important to let ourselves feel our feelings. But when we start feeling like they are the truth of who we are, it becomes a problem. If that is happening, most of the time it's because we have merged with the inner child and our inner adult is not present.

I say most of the time because there are times when we are in catastrophic circumstances and the feelings are truly coming from that present-day experience; it's not the wounded inner child processing old feelings. This may be the case if you are met with a sudden change or loss. Sometimes those feelings really are largely related to the present incident, and you're feeling them as the loving parent.

If you are feeling large feelings, either because they are coming from the wounded inner child or because of the present circumstances, if the inner adult is front and center, you will feel your heart open during the experience. Your inner parent will *always* have a sense of compassion for your inner child and even your inner critic. It may not be overwhelming compassion, but it will be there. And there will not be any judgment.

You might feel like it sucks (it's rare that processing grief is enjoyable), but you will feel held. Similar to how you would if someone you loved was holding you as you cried, that is how you can feel if your loving inner parent is there for you as you are feeling your feelings. At the very least you will feel an allowance, an acceptance that whatever you are feeling is allowed to come up and have a seat at the proverbial table.

This may take some time, and you may get to this place in stages. As you unmerge from the inner child or inner critic, you may first feel only neutral. Then you may feel curious and neutral. Then you may feel curious and have a little bit of compassion. Then at some point you may just feel compassion. And all of these stages can repeat again, depending on what issue you are dealing with. And they may not go in order. Feelings and their processing don't have an order they abide by. Even the stages of grief don't go in the order that Elisabeth Kübler-Ross identified (denial, anger, bargaining, depression, acceptance) all the time. But it's good to have a general roadmap of what might occur and understand that compassion is the place where we can often feel the most transformation. All the inner child wants is to be seen and validated. It's hard to do that if we aren't feeling compassion for them.

Now we know why we want the inner parent to be front and center, why we need them to be able to be objective, and why we need to allow the feelings but not merge with them. Here are some reasons why you may *not* have a loving inner parent guiding you through your life:

- **You weren't able to trust your caretakers.**

- **You have internalized a parent that was very critical.**

- **Your own primary caretaker didn't set boundaries for themselves.**

- **You were taught to be responsible for other people over yourself.**

- Your caretaker was more like a child who didn't take care of themself.

- You had a caretaker who suffered from mental illness, alcoholism, or a debilitating physical illness.

- Your needs, interests, and feelings were only validated if your parent(s) found them valid.

This is far from a complete list, but the general idea is that you had a parent who couldn't give you a good example of being cared for, either because they weren't doing it for themself or they didn't do it for you.

If you felt loved growing up, you may be worried, like many of my clients, that by finding you have a wounded inner child, you are somehow being disloyal to your parents.

This is very important to remember: *you do not need to have "bad" parents or a traumatic history to have a part of you that feels wounded.* It doesn't matter if your feelings were hurt in a way that stuck with you by an otherwise available parent or a dysfunctional one. If the inner child is feeling pain, that means it's valid. Don't forget that it also may have come from someone other than a caretaker. You don't need a notarized note from someone who witnessed the event and can verify that it was "reasonable." If the inner child is feeling it, that's all you need to know. It's simply an indication of where you can use some extra nurturing and attention. And the bonus is that by listening to them, you will get information about what you need to help you with an issue you are tackling today. Judging your inner child as unjustified in its hurt only keeps you stuck.

This is not about blaming the person who cased the pain; it's about taking care of the inner child who feels the hurt now. Sometimes that does involve acknowledging what happened and being mad or hurt. But it's not the focus.

Even wonderful parents cannot be attuned to their children all the time. And the truth is, even *we* can't be the best parent to our inner children *all* the time. But you don't need to be to feel happy and secure. It doesn't require hours and hours of self-reflection. It takes an active relationship with your inner adult, who can simply and honestly say "I see you" from a place of compassion and understanding most of the time. After we have established trust, that can take literally two seconds. The more we can do this, the more we gain a sense of being able to trust ourselves, and the more we hear our needs and feel where we need boundaries.

I had a client who had been in a series of relationships where her partners put her last. She felt wrong wanting to put herself and her needs first, and therefore she didn't question being placed last. Even though her inner child was pretty angry and resentful with what she was allowing in relationships, she ignored that part of herself. Though she was raised with supportive parents who were very loving to her, they did not take care of themselves well. Her father was a workaholic, and her mother put everyone else's needs before her own. My client had no model for how to care for herself or to demonstrate that putting yourself first is important. Because her parents modeled putting themselves last, she was drawn to partners who treated her that way.

She began checking in with her inner child and began to acknowledge how much it hurt her feelings when people took her for granted. She started taking actions based on this realization. She started slowly at first, and it was scary for her, but she started setting boundaries. If her inner child didn't feel safe with someone, she would stop seeing them. If she felt dismissed by her date, first she would acknowledge to her inner child that she heard her, and she eventually would tell the person how she felt or set a boundary and not see them again. Slowly but surely, she began to recognize herself as being worthy and valid. Her relationships changed as she recognized how important it was to prioritize her own needs.

This was challenging, as she had to create the inner parent from the ground up, but it wasn't as challenging as it is for people who don't have any example of love in their environment. She was making big changes on an ancestral level, and that was scary! But she did know what it felt like to be loved unconditionally, so that gave her a framework for what was possible. Her subconscious believed it was possible, which made it easier for her to create that love in her life.

I had another client who knew deeply that she was loved by her father. As a result, she always felt safe with men and rarely had any issues creating loving romantic relationships. However, her mother was a narcissist who devalued my client regularly. Because of this, she grew up feeling less than and had a difficult time in a variety of ways, but particularly with female relationships. The more she was able to check in with her inner child, notice when she was feeling triggered, and give her validation and attention, the more her relationships with women changed.

It's not magic—although it can feel pretty magical—when we see our inner changes reflected around us. It's just a fact that our external environment, including what we tolerate in relationships, is a reflection of how we treat ourselves internally. This "magic" is rooted in the work of treating ourselves differently: no magic wand necessary.

I want to be clear that I am not blaming the victim in any of these situations. Many people deal with issues that are bigger than their relationship with their internal self: racism, homophobia, sexism, and prejudice of any kind are real, systemic conflicts in our world that should be recognized. We live in a culture that was built on othering anyone who isn't straight, white, and male, and that continues to this day. So, for example, there are real obstacles that Black people face that are not a result of inner child wounds. And there are racist, sexist, and homophobic systems in place that are not because of something going on with you internally. I also want to make it clear that it is not your fault if you are being bullied. You cannot change that fact through inner work. But we *can* change many things about our direct environment in terms of whom we interact with and how we react to the people around us. Having a loving inner parent will help you make that change.

CHAPTER FOUR

How Do We Create a Strong, Loving Inner Parent?

N ow that we have some ideas of who the loving inner parent *isn't*, let's focus on what a loving parent is, so that we can start to create one within ourselves that feels as supportive as possible.

What it means to feel we have a loving inner parent will be different for everyone, but the bottom line will be that we will feel seen, validated, and heard, and our main point of view will be centered from a point of compassion. We will feel safe and loved. What might it look like if you had a strong, loving inner parent? This may sound obvious to you, or it may feel vague. Either way, when you ask yourself that question and feel a certain way, that's great information to have. If the idea of having a loving inner parent feels vague, then you know you need to start the process of finding out what makes you feel nurtured. If it feels obvious, that's great! You can start thinking about what actions you can start implementing. But, regardless of what you feel when you ask yourself this question, we can always build on this part of ourselves to make it more expansive and more grounded.

Here are some examples of a strong inner adult to get you thinking about what it can look and feel like.

- **Maybe you don't accomplish something you wanted to achieve, but you are encouraging with yourself and map out a plan to achieve it in a way that feels inspiring rather than discouraging.**

- **If someone close to you is rejecting or rude to you, instead of spending a long time feeling bad about it, you have an inner cheerleader who knows your worth and lets you know it. You find yourself naturally feeling strongly supported, letting yourself express the hurt feelings, and feeling understood.**

- **If you feel scared, you automatically put your hand on your heart or offer yourself some other supportive, nurturing touch and feel supported and nurtured.**

- If you're having a hard time in a relationship, you sort out how you are feeling throughout the day and feel understood by yourself, which gives you the confidence to act on the boundaries that you need.

- You don't feel the need to explain yourself when you set boundaries.

- You don't feel the need to have a "good" reason for not wanting to spend time with someone or do something. Your gut feeling is enough.

- Rather than seeing things as black or white, you are secure enough to see the nuances in people, even those who have hurt you.

- You take breaks and don't push yourself to perform just for the sake of being productive.

- You check in with yourself to see when you need a break and what your motivation is for doing what you're doing.

- You trust your intuition.

- You make time for what brings you joy.

- You accept yourself as being a human who makes mistakes and value all your feelings.

Those are just some examples, but the ways to support yourself are endless. Somehow, just knowing that fact helps me on days when I am so merged with an inner child part that feels that how she feels (bad about herself, sad, believing an old story about her past) is just the *truth*. In other words, days when the "mom globes" are back on in full force.

One way to find out more information about what you need is thinking about something that triggers you, and then thinking about what would make you feel better. For instance, you are on social media and suddenly feel terrible. You check in to pinpoint what you are feeling and realize you got caught up in comparing yourself to others and feel like everyone else is better than you. When you tune in to this concept, you realize what would make you feel better is if the people you admired told you they thought you were amazing and special. *Ding-ding!* Now you know exactly what you need to hear . . . from yourself. We'll get into how to communicate with your inner child in a later chapter, but you can go ahead and try it now in any way that feels good to you. You can imagine those people telling your inner child how special they are, or you can just picture yourself expressing your own self-admiration. Experiment with what feels good. Knowing what you need is a big part of connecting to the inner adult, and communicating can be a bit of trial and error.

There are many ways to show up for ourselves, but if we didn't have a blueprint for it, it can be hard to create that inner resource. That's why I love that we can find so many angles from which to connect to and heal the inner child. On days when I am especially merged with my inner child, I have many ways to connect to her if one isn't creating an immediate softening or healing. Sometimes I will give my clients two or three tools to use if they are in a tough spot.

Finding Your Source of Regulation

In somatic healing, they talk about how in childhood we cannot regulate our own nervous systems. Our bodies are not able to do that yet as children. We are literally not biologically able to. So how do we feel calm and safe? We look to the people around us to help us do that. We *need* them to be what Somatic Experiencing calls our co-regulator.

A co-regulator is someone who helps us soothe our nervous system so that we feel calm and emotionally stable. When I was growing up, Mr. Rogers was an amazing co-regulator for me. It was not great that I didn't have a mom (or a dad who was there often) who could do this for me, but I'm grateful that I and so many other kids were soothed by his radical acceptance. I felt seen by him, even though he wasn't physically present. That's how powerful energy is! I would listen to his records at night, and it would regulate my nervous system to where I felt calm and peaceful enough to fall asleep easily.

Unfortunately, many kids did not have a co-regulator caretaker growing up and thus learned to attempt regulation with people who were in fight, flight, freeze, or fawn mode. When our caretakers consistently reacted to stress by going into one of those modes, that's what we learned to do. Then when it came time to soothe ourselves as adults, we were left without effective tools to do that. Much like my client Marsha from the earlier chapter, the tools we were given to cope were ones that would make us automatically revert to going into fight, flight, freeze, or fawn mode when under stress. They were "tools," but not effective ones. These tools look like maladaptive habits such as making ourselves small, judging others as a way of building ourselves up, and checking out, to name a few. We created inner children who thought they had to go into those habits to survive, because that's how they stayed safe.

What does it look like to have a parent who is locked in their own dysfunctional stress response? Remember Susie, whose mom freaked out when she got a bad grade? That's a great example of the fight response. I have another client whose father shut down when she expressed any big emotion growing up. That's the freeze response. My mother would hang up the phone and sometimes not talk to me for months if I did something she didn't like (e.g., divorce my husband). That's the flight response. And every time I make sure to laugh and smile at someone who is actually making me uncomfortable? That's the fawn response.

If a child drops their ice cream and starts crying, and their parent looks in their eyes and says, "That's really upsetting; I'm so sorry that happened," then the child can experience the pain (and children really feel this as pain) in the presence of a loving person. This helps them feel seen, which in turn allows them to release the pain. It also sets the stage for them to start learning that their needs and emotions matter, and that they can soothe themselves simply by acknowledging their feelings.

If we change that scenario so the parent says, "What's wrong with you? It's just an ice cream! Stop crying! You're over-reacting!" (the fight response), then the child can't release the event. It stays stuck to one degree or another in their physical and energy body. They may feel ashamed, stupid, and/or invalidated. The sadness and shame can't leave their body because they haven't felt it as being resolved. Then they start predicting that this is the response they will get any time they are upset, and they create a habitual stress response (fight, flight, freeze, or fawn).

In this case we are just talking about ice cream and only one event. But when a caretaker repeatedly diminishes a child, simply because they are a child and therefore unable to soothe themself, it sets the stage for the child. This pattern of behavior leads to the child diminishing their feelings in the future, being unable to soothe themself, thinking that their feelings are unimportant, and, perhaps the most destructive, wiring their brain to believe that people aren't there for them and that they are unimportant.

I'm not talking about a parent who is having an off day or a parent who calmly said to the child, "Okay, don't worry about it. It's just an ice cream. We can get more next week.

Stop crying." That wouldn't be ideal, but if it wasn't repeated, it wouldn't be setting up this pattern of the child not being able to soothe themself as an adult.

I'm talking about an environment where the child is repeatedly being dismissed. I'm not saying that every child would have that reaction to that exact circumstance. I'm giving one example of what it looks like to be dismissed as a child and how that behavior will manifest in the child's future emotional life. Every child will come to different conclusions when it comes to parental behavior, depending on the situation. But in the case of repeated diminishment of feelings, those effects are sadly quite common.

Earlier in this chapter, I suggested that you think about a situation that might be triggering to you and think about what would make you feel better. Another way to look at this is to think back to the specific ways in which we didn't get regulated as a child and find clues about what would have made us feel better at that time. If you don't have any childhood memories, that's okay. I like to find many angles to reach the inner child, and if this isn't the one for you, don't worry, there are many more.

If you can, start by thinking about a memory where you didn't get what you needed. Let's say you remember a time when your father ignored you. Investigate that memory for a moment and ask yourself: What is underneath that feeling? Maybe a feeling of not being worthy? A feeling of not being important? Maybe you feel that there is something wrong with you or your father wouldn't have treated you that way. Think about this until you can pinpoint the feeling, like we did with the present-day memory.

Now, what would have made you feel calm and safe back then? Your dad looking in your eyes and apologizing? Giving you a hug? Sitting down together and playing a game after he gave you the attention you needed? What really gives you the feeling of safety in this example?

Those are all clues for two things: what is underneath an old childhood pain that is likely repeating itself in your life now, and ways that you can show up for yourself when that pain shows up now.

Remember that by doing this, you are changing how you show up for yourself not only now, but over time. Creating a secure inner parent for yourself literally changes your neural pathways and influences how you will habitually act in the future. It also creates calm in your nervous system, which is something your body remembers.

One of my clients had a father who would greet boys who came to pick her up for dates by "jokingly" trying to intimidate them. My client knew intellectually that her father meant well and was trying to protect her, but as an adult, she felt guilty about setting boundaries if someone meant well but was still doing something she didn't like. The feeling underneath this instinct was that she was small and didn't have the power to set boundaries or protect herself.

When she understood the underlying feeling, she imagined seeing her father taking her by the hand and saying, "I trust you. And I trust you to protect yourself." This was a lightbulb moment for her: she realized that trust was a theme in her life. When she was triggered about other things, she took that realization and used it to check in to see if trust was playing a part in her reaction. Very often it was! Then she let her inner child know (as we will go over in the next chapter) that she was there for her and would not abandon her. Because she followed that up with actions like setting boundaries and other ways to ensure she would not diminish her feelings, she began to feel the sense of trust she had lacked in a variety of ways in her life.

The person in that example was able to do that through communicating with words to her inner child. But there are many other ways we can feel loved. (Yay! So many ways to help yourself.) I counsel the students in my inner child healing class to look at the ways we feel loved by other people as clues to how we want to feel loved by ourselves.

In his great book *The Five Love Languages*, Gary Chapman outlines five main ways people like to give and receive love. They are words of affirmation, acts of service, gifts, quality time, and physical touch. If you aren't familiar with the concept of love languages, I recommend reading his book for a more in-depth explanation. But the love languages are straightforward enough that you can start now and check in with yourself to see which of them hits home for you.

Once you have a sense of which is the main way you like to receive love, you can start doing that for yourself. If physical touch resonates with you, you can try giving yourself hugs, stroking your arm, or petting your hair (it may sound a little weird, but it really works if you like physical touch). If you're more of an acts of service person, you can do special things for yourself like devoting a section of your room to something you love to do, like meditating or working out. You can choose to clear your calendar once a week to take yourself on a date if you crave quality time. And if words of affirmation make you feel safe and loved, you can speak them aloud to yourself, letting yourself know how proud you are that you're showing up for yourself. And if you like gifts? That's pretty easy: find ways to make or get yourself little tokens of appreciation. There are so many ways we can let ourselves know that we value ourselves.

Sometimes you have to put the cart before the horse. You have to fake it 'til you make it. Even if you feel silly standing across from a mirror and thanking yourself, it's a great way to take the first steps toward cultivating a strong inner parent. If we are not used to loving ourselves in a demonstrative, active way, then it may feel false at first. Or awkward. It's kind of like the beginning of any relationship, where you are challenging yourself to communicate in a new way or setting new rules for how you treat each other. But once you start, you will likely find that it feels really good to be kind to yourself! I know, novel, right?? And a huge bonus is that you will start to have less tolerance for when you or other people cross your boundaries, because you are now really good at showing up for yourself.

Growth always happens on a spiral. I have never once witnessed or experienced a total, complete change that happened all at once. That is completely and totally normal and part of being a human. I have heard of spontaneous spiritual awakenings, like that of Eckhart Tolle. He suddenly understood all of life on a gut level, but I personally have not witnessed this, and he is the only person I have ever heard of this happening to.

I say all this because while doing this work you will grow and change in one area and then realize that there are others that need your attention. Please don't use that as a reason to beat yourself up. We are all on this very human journey. When you are working on yourself consciously, what look like "mistakes" are actually a sign you are growing.

Invite the Loving Inner Parent into Your Life

Simply being compassionate with ourselves brings us out of being merged with the inner child or the inner critic and brings us into the inner parent. Thankfully, the idea that self-love is a silly or superficial thing we don't have time for is becoming less common. Self-love is life changing! I personally have seen many lives changed simply by learning how to compassionately engage in conversation with the part of ourselves that is feeling everything from slightly hurt to devastated. If you had a real child in front of you who had their feelings hurt, you wouldn't think it was silly to comfort them. We need this same comfort as adults. Dismissing this need or judging it only leaves the feelings to stay stuck where they are. They simply don't just disappear, no matter how much we wish they would.

I always counsel people to start this process in small ways at first. It doesn't have to take a lot of time to feel this connection grow. It does take consistency. As I said before, this checking in and acknowledgment can take a few seconds. Books have been written about how small habits done over time can be transformative—even more transformative than large efforts done inconsistently. And this could not be more true with inner child healing.

When you're feeling hurt, simply checking in and saying to yourself "Oh, you're feeling sad; that makes sense, and it really sucks that that happened" can have a huge impact on your mood and your overall sense of inner security and resilience.

My client Mark had a strong inner child voice that wanted him to stay on task at work, no matter what. When he checked in with that part of himself, he learned his inner child thought that Mark would get fired if he didn't accept all tasks, no matter how overworked he was. He worked almost 24/7. When Mark was able to view this inner child compassionately, he saw how much pressure he was putting on himself. He told the inner child that he, the adult, would take care of it, and his inner child could go play. But it turns out that inner child actually wanted to sit at his desk and sort papers! Apparently Mark had asked for an office supply set as a seven-year-old, so this made sense to him. From then on, he would check in on this studious inner child throughout the day, just making sure that he felt okay. Mark said that it was like releasing a stress valve. He liked to work! He just didn't want to feel stressed and overwhelmed. So, by opening up this conversation and inviting in his loving inner parent, he found that being stressed at work didn't feel unmanageable anymore.

I checked in on Mark a month later, and the change had become even more dramatic. He said that he was organically checking things off his to-do list that had been there for months, with no effort. It wasn't even like that inner child part was talking to him—it was just getting done. He also felt comfortable ending his workday and had stopped letting his job leak into his home life. This is the kind of effect that becoming more integrated with the inner child can have.

The other day I was at the store and asked for help from one of the employees, and the man was very rude to me. I wasn't extremely upset about it, but it did irk me. In the past I would have pushed those feelings away and either judged myself for letting such a small thing get to me or judged myself for being hurt at all. I would likely never see this man again in my life, and it wasn't a big deal, so why bother even thinking about it?

The reason is that as much as I could see all the logical reasons very clearly to minimize it, I was in fact bothered, and while I could have ignored it with no consequences, I felt a tug suggesting that my inner child wanted me to address it. Our feelings are not facts, but they don't go away simply by being dismissed. That doesn't mean we have to take every feeling we have seriously. But if we look at emotions from the perspective of the inner child and understand that there is always information attached to how we feel, we can find out helpful information.

When I got to my car after the interaction with the rude grocery store worker, I tuned in to my inner child. I put my hand on my heart and mentally checked in with that part of myself and asked how she was feeling. She responded with a lot of emotion. I was surprised, because intellectually I felt that the interaction was such a small thing, so I didn't think I was that upset. When you are doing this work, you will sometimes find yourself surprised by the reaction you get from yourself, even though it's you. That's because we are often in the habit of glossing over and pushing down our feelings.

I didn't judge myself for having this reaction—that would be the inner critic's job, and shockingly, she had clocked out— so I just listened. My inner child said, "I hate him! He was so mean! Why did he have to treat me like that?" I validated her and (internally in this case) said, "That really hurt your feelings. He *was* really rude." Just hearing that validation softened that part of me completely. I just needed to be heard. Then I, as the inner parent, said, "I'm sorry that happened. You didn't deserve that."

After I did that, my inner child felt very seen and heard, and the feeling dissipated and went away. That freed me up from focusing on how hurt I was. I realized that that man at the grocery store was probably really unhappy if he was rude to strangers for no reason. I found myself having empathy for him. I actually felt compelled to send him love, so I did. Giving myself this love enabled me to see the bigger picture outside of my story of "he was bad, and I was a victim." I'm not saying he should have been rude to me, but altering my perspective helped me let the negative feelings go after I had felt seen and heard by myself.

In the past I would have thought that the only way I could have felt better was if he had apologized to me. Again, this was a small event, so I wouldn't have actually expected him to apologize or even needed an apology. But just the same, he was rude, and I would have thought that I needed him to acknowledge his rudeness to be completely unbothered by it. Now I understand that giving that acknowledgment to myself was much more satisfying.

I also want to note that I used an example of a minor conflict on purpose. This is because many times we will judge ourselves for being put off or hurt by a minor interaction. But whenever that happens, it's always because there's something deeper underneath your initial reaction. In my case, I was raised by someone who was often brash and insensitive about my feelings. Years ago, before I had done work to heal, an interaction like the one I mentioned above would have had me blaming myself. Now that I don't immediately go to self-blame when I feel that way, I experience only some hurt feelings in situations like that, and they aren't very strong. In the future, I may not feel very bad at all.

If this kind of small but still bothersome interaction happens to you, I encourage you to be kind to yourself. If things you deem small are hurting your feelings, your inner child is still holding some pain from the past. It doesn't mean you should be beyond feeling that way. It just means your inner child could use some attention.

Now, could I have happily gone about my day and forgotten about the interaction I had with the rude grocery store employee? Absolutely. And that would have been fine and not a big deal. But by checking in with myself, I am building my inner adult's presence in my life. And that is invaluable. These little ways of showing up for yourself pay off later, in situations that are genuinely, objectively challenging: when you are interacting with a demanding boss, or when a family member pushes your boundaries. You will find that because your inner child knows you care, it won't take as much effort to feel the security of the inner adult in those actually difficult situations.

You don't have to do this every time you experience the slightest hurt. In fact, the more inner adult presence you have, the less you have to say to grow the presence of the inner adult. Eventually, the dialogue you have with yourself could be as simple as "I'm really sorry that guy upset you—you didn't deserve that." And on you go, having built up trust and an inner adult connection that will be there when you deal with bigger issues.

A Note About
Good-Vibes-Only Culture

There is a world in which a minor interaction like the one I described above could have produced this reaction: "I'm happy in my life; this doesn't affect me at all! Peace and love!" Nice, right? But if a sentiment like that isn't coming from a true place of peace, it's not authentic. When we minimize anything we logically know isn't that bad, it's like death by a million papercuts. When we continually judge ourselves for not being positive, it erodes inner trust with our inner child, who is simply trying to communicate their needs with us. When we pressure ourselves to stay positive when we are really feeling anything but, we are forcing ourselves to adhere to an arbitrary set of rules that have nothing to do with our actual emotions. We are instead giving in to the part of ourselves that feels like if we aren't looking at the bright side, we are being silly or mean, or we are wasting our time, or we will fall apart, or we have whatever other reason to ignore our real feelings here. It's different for everyone (and you can talk to that inner child part to find out why), but if you're feeling pressure to act or feel a certain way, investigate why that might be.

Real-World Inner Parent Examples

Another way we can bring our inner parent into our lives in a more concrete way is to look to the people around us that we feel nurtured by. Was there anyone when you were growing up whom you felt safe with? If it wasn't one of your caretakers, what about a teacher, a coach, or a friend's parent? Maybe a family friend or a relative other than your parents? What about celebrities? Thinking about who brings in nurturing helps build the inner parent.

When I started doing this work, I used Mr. Rogers as someone who served as my internal father. When I was having a hard time, I would imagine what Mr. Rogers would have said to me. To me, he's a beautiful example of validation and understanding. When we are looking to create an inner parent, often we will be using the blueprint from our old conditioning, so we have to create a new blueprint. Having as many examples as you can of people who give you this compassionate, supportive feeling is important. Or maybe tough love works better for you. That's great, if that helps you feel supported! (Just make sure it isn't the inner critic masquerading as an inner parent— more on that in the inner critic chapter.) Either way, look for examples of the feeling you want from a parent from as many places as you can.

When I'm upset, I like to imagine a group of these people surrounding my inner child in a circle. Currently on my team are Glennon Doyle, Oprah, Elizabeth Gilbert, Jeff Bridges, and

Mr. Rogers. I imagine them encouraging my inner child and offering support and reassuring words.

As you start to get more familiar with the ways that make you feel loved, you can combine visualizations of your team with your love language. For example, if loving touch makes you feel validated, you can put your hand on your heart while you imagine the best qualities of your ideal inner parent as they communicate with your inner child. This may sound a little complicated, and maybe at first it will feel awkward, but you will get used to it as you practice.

Exercise for Accessing the Inner Parent through the Body

Our bodies can be our first point of entry for many of our experiences. Even though many of us are disconnected from our bodies, we often translate our experiences through our physical forms, even if that's us taking it in and pushing it down. When we purposefully bring our attention there, we can care for ourselves in a profound way.

1. Think of someone or something that makes you feel at peace, someone who helps you feel calm as soon as you are around them. This may be a person, a pet, a plant, even your favorite spot in nature—anything that makes you feel that way.

2. Put your hand on your heart and really sense what it feels like to be with them or at that place. You can also try putting one hand on your heart and one on your belly and see how that feels.

3. See if you can allow that feeling to expand. Don't force it—just watch what happens when you invite it to expand.

4. This may be a very subtle experience. That's okay. It's still actually quite powerful. This is you allowing yourself to embody loving, peaceful energy.

5. Do this as often as you can throughout the day. If you are washing dishes or driving to work, bring up how you feel when you are at your most peaceful.

We contain any feeling that we want to experience. We already have it! I'm not saying we don't need other people, because we do. Other people have the ability to enhance our lives greatly. But we don't need to wait for other people to give us a feeling that we are yearning to have. And certainly not a feeling of being parented and nurtured.

If you were raised in an environment where that was absent, it can feel like you don't deserve it or that it doesn't exist. But by experiencing it firsthand from yourself, you can start to feel it to believe it.

Consistency is critically important in doing these types of activities to connect you with your inner parent and inner child. The exercise given here could take three minutes. If you do that every day, you will likely begin to notice that feeling popping up organically. You will also likely start to spontaneously get ideas for how to give yourself what you need. Just like in the past when you were paying attention to past programming in terms of what *doesn't* make you feel good, you can now create new ways of giving yourself what you do need when you pay attention to your inner parent.

Reprogramming the Subconscious

From the time we are born until we are around seven years old, our brain waves are in the alpha and theta state. This is the same state that your brain is in now as an adult when it's under hypnosis or meditation. These brain waves are active when you walk in nature and feel immersed in it, in the shower, and just before you fall asleep. This state of mind occurs when you let go of the logical mind and are open enough to receive clear connection to your intuition.

When we are children, our brain is absorbing everything around us, and its main objective is to keep us safe. It is actively looking for and downloading what we need to do to create safety. This includes important information about how we relate to others, how we experience their relating to us (Do we have to earn love? Do we have to please or fight for it?), what we do to keep ourselves safe (fight, flight, freeze, or fawn), and how and if we can trust people, to name a few things.

To be clear, "safe" to the brain means familiar. It is wiring how you should relate to others based on the blueprint of how your family interacted with each other. The brain doesn't see "safe" as finding new, healthier relationships, because those would be unfamiliar to a child who grew up in dysfunction.

This is all done in this hypnotic state. After the age of seven, when our brain leaves the theta state, all the information gets stored in our subconscious, where then as adults we draw on that information habitually. From then on, when we meet a potential partner, interact with anyone, or attempt to stretch past our comfort zone, our brain takes most of its information from all of that potent time as a child and uses it to help us determine how to behave to feel safe around this person. If this person feels familiar, the programming is especially easy to revert to.

Since our brain is designed to keep us safe, it's not there to be on the lookout for how we can change up patterns that aren't working for us emotionally and that will stretch us and temporarily make us feel uncomfortable or scared. That's up to our higher selves, our inner parent, our intelligence in our bodies and intuition. Of course we use the brain for many vital things, but we can't just think our way out of entrenched emotional patterns. If we do this, we are going to keep hitting our heads against the wall, not getting much traction. We are going to keep doing what we learned in childhood to keep us safe.

Part of being a helpful inner parent is noticing when the brain is still operating from old programming to make decisions about whom you should be in close relationship with, how you feel people will react to you, whom you should open up to, and much more. Once you notice that you are reacting to people and situations from that perspective, you can start the process of bringing your inner child into the present to show it that you are here now and it can be different. You can start reprogramming the subconscious to take people in anew.

One way to change how the brain automatically takes in information is to reprogram it through visualization in meditation. The inner child meditation in the first chapter is one way to do that. Any meditation where you examine a past event that made you look at yourself in a harmful way and then imagine it going in a way that feels healing is reprogramming your subconscious.

Take social media. Many people post something and then immediately start looking at how many people liked it or commented. They are using social media as a way to prove that they are okay and safe, like they may have had to do in childhood. Social media sometimes delivers. But really, it's a vehicle in this case: a way for us to see where our inner child is hoping something external will prove to us that we are lovable. Or valid. Or achieving enough. Or that there isn't something wrong with us.

If you were to go back in time and consider where that feeling of needing validation first came from, you might discover that, for instance, your mother was not easy to please, and you were constantly in a situation where you were hoping to get her approval. Your subconscious had been programmed with the belief that to stay safe, you needed her approval. But because her approval was so hit-or-miss, you were trained to be on the lookout for her reaction to know how you should feel about yourself. Flash forward to the present day: you go on Instagram, and suddenly those feelings come rushing back. You feel overcome with the need for that same approval, because your programming tells you that it will help you to feel comforted.

The trick with social media is to stop this process. For example, try doing a meditation or visualization where you imagine getting your mother's approval. Imagine the feeling of being affirmed and validated, and then follow that up with an acknowledgment directed to your inner child, letting them know you approve of them now, no matter how many likes your post received. What matters is that you choose yourself. Do it frequently enough and you will find that the feeling of needing external validation will begin to feel less intense. If you do this enough, it may even go away completely.

Your brain is straightforward in this way. Kind of like sea turtles who instinctually move toward the ocean after hatching, your brain goes on autopilot, heading straight toward that childhood programming it is so familiar with. *Familiar = safety* to your brain, so it's driven to get there. In order to change that programming, first you have to recognize what the subconscious has latched onto because it thinks it will keep you safe. After you have figured that out, you can work on changing it. But this doesn't mean it's *easy* to change.

At first, untangling this association may not look like change at all. A strong inner parent will look different for everyone. Here is how I have seen growth manifest after the development of a strong inner parent:

1. Witnessing the thing you want to change (inner parent initiates this).

2. Having realizations about where it came from in the first place (higher self/inner parent).

3. Doing the thing again (for example, engaging in the behavior you wish you could stop, or feeling triggered) and experiencing it a little differently because the inner parent was in and out.

4. Doing the thing again and being hard on yourself and feeling lost because the inner parent is gone.

5. Witnessing again (inner parent comes back).

6. Having more realizations (higher self/inner parent is present).

7. Doing work to change this process.

8. Feeling more empowered, not engaging in the thing, and even creating new reactions and behaviors (inner parent more consistently showing up).

9. Getting triggered again and being a little less hard on yourself (inner parent coming in and leaving again).

10. Finally, not engaging in the thing, and maybe not even reacting or feeling bad about it (inner parent present).

If the association comes up again in a different circumstance, this whole pattern could repeat, but quickly and with less intensity. Or it may get shortened to just realizing it's happening and not engaging, instead behaving in the new, expansive way that you have reprogrammed yourself to achieve.

Obviously, this is not a be-all and end-all description of growth, but it's an example of a process I see happening all the time and experience myself.

As I'll likely repeat throughout this book, remember that growth is a spiral, and humans do not grow in a straight line. It would be inhuman to never feel like you are going backward. But trust me, it is completely normal. This means that you can be extra kind to yourself when you thought you had grown past something and then are challenged with it again. For instance, if you are working on getting better at setting boundaries, you will have days when you state what you need and days when you say yes when you want to say no. This is part of the process.

You may connect to your inner child and find that, in certain situations, they need you to reassure them over time. This is also part of the growth process and is totally normal. It's helpful to treat this as such and not as if you are failing or as if they are needy. In some cases, the inner child has been building up the way they feel for years, so it makes sense that they may need reminding of whatever lesson you are learning.

As you start to grow your loving inner parent, one thing you can consistently do is check in: *Am I feeling compassion for a part of me that is struggling? Or do I feel like I am my inner child or critic?* If you are feeling compassion, that means the inner parent is there. If you aren't, then you are merged with the inner child or the inner critic.

Journal Prompts to Connect to Your Loving Inner Adult

Take some time to think about your ideal inner parent with these journal prompts. If you don't like journaling, you can also get into a comfortable position, close your eyes, and feel into the answers, but I encourage you to journal. Writing things down helps us access even more information than when we ruminate over them. Just like how when you talk or write about a dream you remember more about it than if you were just thinking about it, journaling will help you more than merely thinking about your ideal inner parent in this exercise.

To make this a somatic experience, remember to breathe and connect to your whole body when you are considering each prompt. Your inner adult is heart centered and uses your entire body. When you connect with your body, you can connect to your inner adult more easily.

- What qualities do you find most nurturing when you are feeling sad or upset? For example, do you want to simply be heard and listened to? Or do you prefer touch? Or maybe it feels best to have someone solution-oriented help you with your problem. Maybe what you need changes from situation to situation. Take a moment and think about what makes you feel nurtured.

- Consider the five love languages: physical touch, words of affirmation, gifts, acts of service, and quality time. Think about how you like to receive love from a parent.

- What does it mean to you to feel grounded and in your body? Can you describe it or what you need to get there?

- How does it feel to be seen and validated? Write about a time when you felt this.

- Write about an imaginary experience in which you feel seen and validated.

- Think about a person who exudes this loving inner parent to you, whether it's someone you know personally or not. Describe what you feel when you think of this person.

Quick Hack for Connecting
to the Inner Adult

One of my clients has a brilliant approach: she has a theme song for her inner adult that she puts on in the morning to help her connect to it. The one she is using now is "Higher Love" by Steve Winwood. This helps her feel uplifted and connected to the idea of being with a "higher" loving part of herself. Music is such a powerful way to shift our moods and mindset quickly, partly because it connects us to our body and gets us out of our heads. It's helpful to do this first thing in the morning to establish this feeling right away.

Your senses are incredibly powerful, and using all five senses when changing old programming can create a huge impact. Whenever I smell Polo cologne, my mind goes right back to my boyfriend in high school who wore it. When you hear a song that has a sentimental attachment to it, it's so easy to be taken back to the time period when you formed those memories. So consider using taste, smell, touch, sound, and sight for connecting to the higher part of yourself that can get lost in programming that is not true.

Here are some questions for you:

- Is there a smell that makes you feel grounded or joyful? Perfume is a great way to instantly feel connected to your inner adult.

- Is there a fabric that calms you instantly when you touch it? Wear an article of clothing made with that fabric when you have to set a boundary you are anxious about or before you deliver a speech at a work.

- What song makes you feel powerful? Make that your theme song for the week or year.

- Is there a certain location that brings you back into your body when you go there or look out at it? I am lucky enough to live in the mountains and feel relaxed just looking out my window. But if you aren't in that situation, find a picture of a place that makes you feel rejuvenated.

- What food or drink makes you feel soothed? There's a reason we call it comfort food. Taste is one of the senses that can help bring us back to ourselves. I am completely against moralizing food choices, so I'm not demonizing comfort eating. If you're eating it consciously and it's what you want, go for it! But I also think that if it's going to send your inner child into a spiral, then that's great information and not the best idea for one of your ways to connect quickly to your inner adult.

CHAPTER FIVE

The Inner Critic

et's all take a deep breath as we start this chapter, because
even the idea of the inner critic can bring up a lot of anxiety and resistance. No one wants to talk to a bully, and that is
no different if it's living inside of ourselves. But as the inner
parent chapter covered, when we are in a state of compassion,
there's nothing we can't conquer. (Cue the *Rocky* soundtrack!)

There's even more good news. The inner critic isn't exactly
the villain you may be imagining: it's simply a misguided part
of ourselves that is actually trying to help us. Isn't that amazing? Truly, this fills me with hope and gratitude that our psyche
was designed to help us, not hurt us.

The inner critic wants to be seen, just like the inner child does, and is, in fact, a part of the inner child. After getting to know the inner critic, we are likely to find that it is a child or teenage part of ourselves, because we learned whatever tactic they are using when we were that young. So even though the feisty inner critic appears to be different from the hurt inner child, it really is just a child part that needs your love and attention as much as the wounded inner child does.

Often, the critic can appear like a parent who was less than supportive (or even abusive), or like a supportive parent who wasn't kind to themself. It's no wonder the inner critic doesn't seem like they are on our side. And it's true that they are definitely not on the same page as the inner parent. But by investigating a little further, we can see their true motivation and get them aligned with the inner parent.

It may be surprising to learn that having a supportive parent who is not kind to themself can leave you with the same dysfunctional tools as someone who had a critical parent. We absorb so much as children in terms of how to treat ourselves, and if we don't have a model for someone treating themself well, we may not get the information for how to do it. Their encouraging us to be kind to ourselves may not feel believable if we never see them doing it for themselves. Or we may ultimately feel like it's not okay to set boundaries or talk kindly to ourselves because our role model didn't do it. So if you had a supportive parent but a loud inner critic, this is good to be aware of.

The inner critic is often just trying to protect us from putting ourselves out there and being vulnerable, and they're often quite clever in the ways that they do this. They can create a lot of energy to feel powerful (although that energy often looks like criticism) and sometimes seemingly duplicate the energy of a dysfunctional parent for various reasons, all rooted in protection. Maybe we can even learn to value the hard effort that the inner critic is putting forth in order to serve us. This can help us get to compassion easier.

If we understand that we can take out the distraction of criticism by engaging in compassionate communication with our inner critic, it can help us feel like we aren't being run by them. By being a sacred witness, from the seat of compassion, we can find out their story and find out how to integrate them in a helpful way.

In Japan there is a practice in pottery called *kintsugi* that uses liquid gold or silver to bind broken pieces. When this is done, the precious, beautiful metal shows up where the cracks were, highlighting them. In this way, attention is called to the brokenness and, at the same time, its value is shown. I think about this process sometimes when I talk with my and my clients' inner critics. On the one hand, they are being mean and even destructive, but on the other hand, they have so much to offer us. Most of the time they are just scared and needing our love.

This is a dynamic and sometimes complicated relationship that deserves our attention. We deserve to have a relationship with *all* of the parts of ourselves, including the parts that have gotten turned around and misdirected at some point. We can learn how to stay centered while we handle this dynamic, just like we would with any other relationship in our lives that is worth having. And I hope that by the end of this chapter, you will feel like it truly is worth having.

For my client Jeremy, the inner critic came in a pair with his wounded inner child. The inner critic was actually coming in to protect the inner child. Jeremy would experience the feeling of the inner child but hear the dominating voice of the inner critic.

Jeremy would often feel drained and depressed about a work relationship when he was being asked to do more than was reasonable. When he checked in with his inner child, he saw that the inner child felt like he had no way out, like he wanted to stop working at an out-of-control pace but felt he wasn't allowed to. He was afraid that if he didn't do absolutely everything that was asked of him, Jeremy would be rejected and fired. When Jeremy gave the inner child compassion, he then heard the inner critic chime in right away. This is because the inner critic wasn't comfortable with the inner child feeling heard. The inner critic felt he had to drive my client to do what he was expected to do at work in order to avoid rejection.

First, Jeremy heard the inner critic out, but then he told the inner critic that, as the inner parent, it was Jeremy's job to manage people's expectations and that *he* could determine if they were unreasonable or not. He didn't need criticism or a feeling of dread or harshness to do that. Jeremy asked the inner critic if he would talk to Jeremy with respect and help him specifically with prioritizing things. The inner critic seemed dubious that my client would listen to him, but was willing to give it a shot.

What happened next was a true testament to what happens when you integrate the inner critic's voice. After a lifetime of dealing with harsh inner criticism, Jeremy realized he was hearing from the inner critic less frequently. If he did sense some harshness from that part of himself, he could quickly check in, and it would soften. And the most remarkable change was that my client started being able to initiate interactions with authority figures more easily. For example, he had been meaning to send an email to his boss for months in which he explicitly outlined what needed to change and what he would no longer do at work. He had been putting it off for several reasons: he didn't feel like it was a good time, he felt embarrassed to ask for what he needed, and he felt like he wasn't worthy of his boss's consideration. But after his conversation with his inner critic, he wrote the email and was able to get specific in a way he never could before. He didn't even have a conscious conversation with the inner critic before writing the email—he just wrote it. He said it happened so easily that he didn't even notice the connection between having had that conversation with the inner critic and being able to write the email until later.

This is an example of how even the parts of ourselves that act at complete cross purposes with us actually want to help. It makes me feel the profound connection we have with our energy bodies, knowing that even when, for instance, the chakras are blocked, it's not happening to hurt us. The energy just needs some attention, understanding, and care for it to move, so we can feel more integrated.

It can be helpful to check in when you feel hurt or reactive, because it means the wounded inner child has been activated in some way. Because the inner critic is closely linked with the inner child, it could mean that some negative dynamic is playing out that should be investigated. For Jeremy, the inner critic rushes in anytime the inner child feels hurt to try to blow out the fire, but ends up making it worse.

For instance, you may be feeling anxious about emailing a friend to let them know you can't make it to their party, but then you start criticizing yourself for procrastinating on the reply. In this case, your inner child is scared to reply because they're worried your friend will be mad at them. And then your inner critic comes in thinking that if they berate you, you'll reply faster, and then your friend won't be mad at you for never replying. When you center your loving inner parent, you can let your inner critic and inner child know that you will only give time to friends who truly value you, and that if anyone would cut you off because of a delayed email or because you couldn't make it to their party, then they weren't worth your friendship. But you could remind your critic that you do like to send timely replies, so if they want to remind you that it is important to be prompt with replies, that's appreciated—as long as they do it in a supportive manner.

This may sound like a lot of work, but it can become effortless. If you repeat this scenario consistently and continue to work with your inner critic, you will find that you don't need to have an actual conversation every time conflict happens, because you addressed the concerns earlier. As with any other relationship, if it's been rocky, it will take some effort to heal it. But you live with yourself for your entire life, and that effort is so worth it.

Naming Your Inner Critic

Some people name their inner critic. This can be useful because it helps us to feel the inner critic's presence viscerally. It reminds us that we are not our critic, but that rather, they are a part of us. However, I caution you to consider this technique only after you have had a loving connection with your critic so that the act of giving it a name is coming from a place of collaboration, not conflict. If you haven't developed this connection, it's tempting to give your critic a snarky or ugly name. Instead, pick something that evokes a feeling of compassion and respect. Or, at the very least, just pick something neutral. I personally don't have names for my various inner child parts, but I have had clients assign them names based on a feeling. My husband has a teenage part of himself that developed at a rebellious stage of his life. When talking to his inner critic, my husband clearly hears that his inner critic's name is Rickshaw.

It makes him laugh because it is so random, which helps keep things light, and it helps him to clearly identify the rebellious teen, who is often very skeptical of anything new that he is trying, including inner child work.

This brings up an important point: sometimes you *will* have an inner critic who is skeptical of doing this work, and it's important to hear them out. My husband listened to his skeptical inner critic's concerns and made sure that he felt validated and not pushed aside. In my husband's case, his inner critic (it does feel weird for *me* to call him Rickshaw) was worried that he was falling into a trap like he viewed my husband's religious childhood to be. My husband assured his inner critic that he would listen to his concerns and would act on anything if he felt that it was troublesome. If he hadn't done that, they would have been locked in a power struggle just like they were before my husband started consciously talking to him.

And you may have been surprised to learn that my husband *heard* his inner critic. This is pretty common. Remember that we hear ourselves talk all day long—we just don't usually identify the voices as being separate parts. As I mentioned before, hearing those separate parts of ourselves has been pathologized, when in fact it's perfectly normal. So you may hear your inner child, you may just get a feeling of what they are needing, or you may even visualize them very clearly. However you do it is correct.

In terms of the inner critic, before we get familiar with them, we may have a hard time identifying how they show up in our lives *unless* we hear them in a clear, critical voice. I think most of us have the idea that the inner critic would be obvious and easy to spot, that they sound like "Expletive, expletive, that was stupid, expletive." And sometimes that is true. (I really hope that changes soon if that's you!) But most of the time I would say that the inner critic does not show up as an overtly critical voice—it can show up in more oblique ways. For example, when the inner critic is very loud, you might be doing things like:

- **Obsessing, trying to figure things out in a way that isn't helpful.**

- **Getting lost in a social media wormhole, comparing yourself to other people.**

- **Appearing very much like a parent managing your life but with a tone, energy, or urgency that is harsh.**

- **Feeling a sense of "why bother?"**

- **Feeling dread or disgust, or a heaviness that you can't identify.**

- **Procrastinating or lashing out at people. Maybe even blaming them, kind of like a child having a tantrum.**

One way to get more familiar with your inner critic is to ask yourself where you feel your reaction in your body. If you notice that you have disconnected from your body, that you are only in your head and are overthinking, that is a clue that the inner critic may be active. It might be the inner child too, but you are definitely not centered in the inner parent.

When you are stuck in your head, it's so important to connect to your body. This opens you up to the resources that your spirit and body have that you lose access to when you are busy judging yourself.

To give yourself energetic space away from your inner critic, get out in nature, dance, go for a walk or a drive, shower, do art, listen to music, move your body, or anything that helps you to feel connected to your whole self. These activities help us find other solutions when we might have spent the time criticizing ourselves. They also help us affirm to our inner child that we care and that we, as the inner adult, are present. Building this kind of trust is transformational in so many ways, but particularly when it comes to the inner critic. It tells our inner child that we won't succumb to the harmful patterns the inner critic has taken up. And it gives us the breathing room we need to center into the loving inner parent and talk to the inner critic from a place of understanding.

The Inner Critic Embodying Your Critical Parent

Sometimes the inner critic sounds exactly like one of your caretakers who was critical or abusive. Many years ago, after telling a therapist that I couldn't divorce how I felt about myself from the things my mom said to me, she said, "You need an exorcism." She was kidding (as far as I know!), but at the time, I really did wish I could just banish my mom's voice from my head. It would have been great to just delete all the files that contained the criticisms from my mother so I could stop hearing them all day long.

In some ways, it is possible to do that with reprogramming or hypnosis. You can go back and give yourself the childhood you needed in a way that can override the programming you received. Showing up consistently as the inner loving parent is another way to do this.

Another way to look at this is that your inner critic may have adopted the voice of the critical caretaker as a way to attack you before you are attacked in the outside world in a similar way. Remember, your inner critic's ultimate goal is safety, so by berating you in the voice of that angry caretaker, your critic is trying to keep you from being attacked by others like them in your life. Or your critic is trying to prepare you in case this happens again. It's not the most logical solution, but it works in the sense that it prevents you from leaving your comfort zone—it's too painful and too scary to do unfamiliar things when you know you're just going to get yelled at. But the truth is, all this critical inner voice really does is beat us down and keep us in the same energetic pattern and traveling the same uncomfortable neuropathways. The unpleasant voice of the critic forces us to relive experiences that are probably not even happening anymore. When we have our heads down and our mind focused on all the ways we may have screwed up, or on the reasons we need to be hypervigilant, the sad fact is that we are missing out on the rest of our lives. We are missing possibilities for new solutions and new ways to approach our lives that may serve us. That's why it's so important to find out what your inner critic *really* needs, because they are, in reality, a part of yourself. If we rescue them, we rescue ourselves.

As with the inner child, the only way you can know the inner critic's motivation is to talk to them and figure out what they need. We will go into the details of how to do that in the next chapter, but for now you can start by becoming aware of that voice as a *part* of you, not the all-encompassing fact of your existence. Breathing in and accessing self-compassion, you can try to see this part of yourself as wanting the best for you. From that place, ask them what they need. If they are willing to talk to you, then you can work together.

If this part of you seems stuck in their role, ask if this pattern or energy is yours, your parents, or someone else's. This may sound strange, but sometimes we adopt a parent's energy (and even more so, an ancestral energy) as a way to have any kind of interior parent. This is where energy healing can help a lot.

Energy Healing and the Inner Critic

I had a client named Wren who asked me to talk to her mother, who had passed. They had a difficult relationship when her mother was alive, and Wren was looking for some clarity. Her mother made very clear what I have often seen and sensed from my own ancestral line: a dark, cloudy energy. Wren's mother indicated that it was full of a feeling of dread and discontent and that it had been given to her by her mother, and her mother had gotten it from her grandfather.

I saw that when Wren was little, she unconsciously took on that energy as a way to fit in with the rest of the family, who had all taken it on themselves. She didn't feel comfortable with it, but she also didn't feel safe without this "coat" of family energy. In fact, when she thought about letting it go, it felt like losing her family.

In her childhood, Wren had to find a way to manage this energy. She developed a part of herself that assumed blame for this heaviness. As a result, she became locked into a family dynamic of competition that involved not only her mother but also her sisters. I could see that although the energy was not hers, she had created a part of herself that was in charge of managing it, so it felt very much like it was hers.

Since we were working with her mother directly, I had Wren imagine taking the energy and handing it back to her mother. Wren's mother was actually glad to take back the energy she had handed to Wren so that she could heal it. After Wren's mother received this energy, she in turn handed it back to Wren's grandmother, who handed it back to her father. I saw him hand it back to someone else, and eventually all of the energy was swooped into a vacuum of light.

After this exchange, Wren felt much lighter—as did her mother, who thanked us. At that point, I helped Wren talk to her inner child, who had been managing this energy all alone. I asked her if she needed anything and was told that she needed some reassurance that Wren didn't need her help shouldering the burden of this dark, stormy family energy anymore. What Wren's inner child really wanted was to go play and be free—she had spent so many years focusing on dealing with this burden and was exhausted and depleted. Wren's inner child asked her to make time for more play, which she agreed to.

If you have a sense that you are holding on to family energy, try a similar technique. It will be good for you, but you will also be doing your ancestors a favor, as a family's energy can become stuck. By releasing yourself from the burden of shouldering so much pain, you are also allowing your entire family line to free it from their own energy field. And if this sounds too far-fetched or "woo-woo" for you, you don't have to be confident that this is happening to do it. You can simply hold the intention that you are giving yourself and your ancestors freedom from the responsibility of carrying pain, imagining that intention coming from a place of healing and compassion.

To do this, imagine the person whose negative voice may function as your inner critic. Say to them "I'm handing this back to you" or anything else that feels right. You will then see your parent handing it backward in a line to their parent (or whoever feels right) and so on and so on. It's completely possible that this image may look different for you. Let your mind wander into whatever situation makes sense to you in this scenario. You might be surprised to see who emerges when you think of your inner critic and, when you hand energy back to that person, whom they in turn pass it along to. Remember that however you do this exercise, you are doing it perfectly. When it is done, and your family members have all handed back their energy, imagine a big light at the end of this chain of people, or a vacuum that sucks up the light, and see all these people and the energy they have been carrying gently and easily go into it.

I like to imagine all of the energy that originated with the inner critic and all of my ancestors being gently absorbed by the light. This doesn't mean these family members have disappeared forever, just that that energy pattern they were perpetuating is getting cleaned and recycled.

When you hand energy back to the caregiver who may have berated you, you don't have to know for sure that it originated with them. If you are the child (adopted or biological) of your caretaker, you will have taken on some of their energy if they were responsible for raising you at all. So handing back that energy is a gift to them, and is healing for everyone. There is no such thing as bad energy—just energy that is not serving you. Sometimes energy that is not serving you can feel heavy, and if you are giving it a negative intention, it can feel bad. But when you are offering energy with compassion and sending it to the light, it is a positive experience that helps everyone.

Mark Wolynn, in his book *It Didn't Start with You*, cites many scientific studies that prove we inherit family traits like anxiety and depression. For example, a grandparent who experienced severe depression can transfer that genetically to their grandchild. So when we are feeling things are not ours, it is really true that they may not be!

One more technique can be useful if you are experiencing guilt about handing energy back. My guides shared this with me, and many of my clients have since found it to be effective:

1. Close your eyes and get in touch with what you are feeling.

2. Imagine you are surrounded by light, and, if you like, ask for a guide that is there for only your highest good to be with you.

3. Imagine a tube, like a garbage chute but full of light, next to you.

4. Then imagine taking the energy out of your body and letting the tube suck it up and deliver it wherever it belongs. Sometimes if we don't actually envision

the person it's going to, it can be easier to let energy go. As long as our intentions are for it to go back to its rightful home, we are releasing the energy in an ethical way.

5. When you are done, fill up with light.

Chakra Healing for the Inner Critic

We can also work directly with our chakras when we feel the inner critic is overactive. Many times, the inner critic lives in the third chakra, which is our personal will center and often the place of power struggles. But it can also show up in a variety of ways, sometimes even appearing like the inner child, sometimes like a parent, sometimes like a taskmaster, and in many other roles. Finding the inner critic can be tricky, and sometimes by tuning in to which chakra we are feeling it from, we can identify better what its real needs are.

Thinking about the inner critic, where do you feel them? In what part of your body? Let's say you are imagining they are in your stomach. Your third chakra is located there. Imagine putting a drop of light into that chakra, and imagine it whirling around there like a washing machine. Imagine any energy you don't want from that chakra going into a big sun six feet in front of your body. See or sense it burning off the energy, and then once again put light into that chakra.

You can also do the same technique with all of the seven chakras, simply holding the intention to clear out the energy that you are associating with the inner critic. For instance, if you are feeling a lot of dread, start with the first chakra at the base of your spine and imagine putting that drop of light in it. Hold the intention that any dread energy is clearing out and going into the sun. Do that with each chakra. When you are done, fill up with light.

Doing visualizations like this is an effective way to clear your energy body so that you can hear your own information more distinctly. We often want to push our inner critic into the shadows and reject them because they come off as harsh or unkind. When we do this kind of energy healing, we *are* clearing out the old, but we are doing it in a way of releasing anything that isn't serving us. Sometimes we can get bogged down by the old energy, and when we feel a little less burdened we are more able to hear what that inner critic voice was trying to tell us. Or maybe they just needed to feel a sense of connection with you, and that healing did the trick.

The comment I hear most from clients after they do this visualization is that they feel lighter. This is because they have been holding old patterns and thoughts in their energy field, and we have cleaned it out in the session. Even though we have talked about heavy topics, their energy isn't holding it as much, so they have more capacity to look at whatever is ready to be looked at.

The Shadow and the Inner Critic

The concept of the shadow is originally from Carl Jung—the same psychologist who wrote about the inner child. When we reject parts of ourselves, we push them into the shadows of our psyche (or the unconscious), and all of that material ends up coming out in a variety of ways—it can really rule our lives. Or, as Jung more succinctly put it: "Until you make the unconscious conscious, it will direct your life and you will call it *fate*."

Here are some of the ways the shadow shows up:

- **You reject the part of you that wants people to admire you, so you judge anyone who posts selfies on social media.**

- **You never really enjoy sex because you unconsciously believe that it's shameful, but consciously you tell yourself that sex just isn't your thing.**

- **You think that spending money on yourself is greedy, so you never have the things you need but could afford and resent people who do.**

- **You tell yourself it's the right thing to do to give more than you want to in relationships and therefore have only imbalanced relationships.**

All of these examples, and pretty much anywhere the shadow shows up, involve a heavy dose of the inner critic. I had a client who found herself obsessing about her brother's girlfriend. She didn't like her, and she told me she just wanted to stop worrying about it. The example she gave was one I used here: the girlfriend was "flaunting herself" on social media, and it rubbed my client the wrong way.

When we looked at her energy, we were able to identify her inner child, who was criticized for celebrating her accomplishments. When she came home after winning second place in the spelling bee and told her dad how proud she was, he gave her a dismissive look and told her not to get carried away with herself. That was reinforced throughout her childhood, as she was told she was being a "showoff" or "acting like a diva" when she would speak of anything she felt good about accomplishing.

She carried that energy of judgment with her, and it would come out in ways she didn't realize. She told me that people found her to be off-putting, and when I looked at it, I saw that they unconsciously felt judged by her. This was her shadow expressing itself.

Anytime she felt excited or proud, the inner critic would rush in to remind her that she could not feel that under any circumstances. Of course the inner critic does not say that kindly, so it would come out like "Don't be gross" or a feeling of shame. Because she felt that heavy judgment energy about herself (the inner child), she would criticize other people when they would express feeling good about themselves.

Remember that it's important to be aware that when we have these judgments in the shadows, they can appear as critical words or come out as feeling bad about yourself. Especially if you have set a boundary around not talking critically to yourself, those judgments can come out sideways as a feeling of low self-worth.

In the session with my client, we had her talk to her inner critic, and it quickly became clear that the intensity around getting her to be quiet about her accomplishments ("just shut up already!") was masking the intention to stay small. As soon as she looked at it with compassion, the clarity around feeling incredibly intimidated by her father was what stood out. The inner critic was trying to avoid having my client be a target again. I asked my client to see if the inner critic felt like her dad's opinion was important to her. When she did, she found out that the inner critic (who was an adolescent) actually didn't respect him at all and saw him as having very "loud" ideas that had no backing and that she didn't believe in. Having this information allowed her to detach from the worldview that the inner critic was trying to protect her from.

After that, we got into redirecting the inner critic to doing something that was helpful. My client told her inner critic that it would be more helpful to use her energy for reminding her that her dad's worldview was not something she cared about and that it wasn't the present reality. Now that they had this connection, the inner critic was able to do this.

That is just one example of how shadowy material like insecurity and shame have much more power when you try not to look at them. We always have good reasons for doing this, but just like the child who is afraid of the monster in the closet, our inner child parts are fearing a monster that we'll see is not so scary when we open the door and greet it with compassion.

That is not to say our experiences—the ones from which the shadow were generated—were never scary. Many of us had some pretty real monsters in our lives. But when we consciously connect to the inner child or critic that lives in the shadow, we can bring them into the present time and feel—not just know intellectually—that we now have tools to handle them.

Journal Prompts for
Working with the Shadow

- What feeling do you most hate feeling (for example, shame, embarrassment, self-disgust)? Where are you feeling that in your life now?

- Where do you find yourself shrinking or making yourself small? Whom do you do this with?

- Who annoys you? What is it about them that you really can't stand?

- Who are you jealous of? What is it underneath that you really wish you had?

- What word or quality would you never want to be associated with? If you have a hard time with this, think of the best thing someone could ever call you. Then think of the opposite of that.

CHAPTER SIX

Communicating with Your Inner Child

I use three main techniques to connect with the inner child. I recommend trying them all and seeing which has the most impact for you or feels the best. On paper, it may seem like one technique or the other is the obvious choice, but when you do all three, you may find that one of the ones you might have passed over will feel more powerful than you'd thought.

When you're trying these techniques, try not to overthink. It is natural that you might get a little lost in your own head here, as we are not taught to talk to ourselves in the way I'm about to describe. But if you notice kids going about their business, you'll see that they often talk to themselves or have imaginary friends that they use to work out issues going on internally. We are trained out of this as we grow up—and it's too bad that we are.

It's common to rely on analysis as a defense mechanism. If you grew up in an environment where you felt you had to figure everyone out in order to feel safe—for example, if you felt like you had to stay one step ahead of an unreliable or abusive primary caretaker—you probably developed a habit of going into your head and analyzing the situation instead of feeling your feelings. I get it! When I first went to therapy at age twenty-one, my therapist handed me a list of feelings, because when I felt anything, I described it as "weird."

She was trying to get me to identify exactly what was going on with me instead of rejecting those emotions because they didn't logically make sense. Feeling feelings was scary, and overanalyzing everything to death gave me the illusion of control, which saved me from dealing with all those pesky "weird" feelings. Take this opportunity to let your emotions happen, and don't rush to push them away simply because they may not entirely make sense.

Intellectualizing everything gives you only an illusion of control. When we go into our heads to analyze instead of feeling, we are pressing "pause" on the situation. We rarely come to any real conclusions when we tell ourselves not to feel—we are just putting ourselves into purgatory, a place where we can't process what has happened but still somehow feel terrible. When we don't feel our feelings in the moment, we experience a different kind of pain—the pain of feeling separate from our-selves. The feelings can pass, but only if we allow them to come through first.

Let's start the communication to give you some peace.

Meditative Connection

Right now, my favorite way of communicating with my inner child is through meditation. There is no one best way to feel most connected to your inner child, but I find that many people enjoy meditative connection.

You'll probably want to do this with your eyes closed, but you can't do that and read this at the same time, so walk your-self through it first with eyes open. And sometimes I do like to do it with my eyes open, too.

First, tune in to a part of you that feels upset or triggered. If you're just starting out, you may want to do this with an issue that is not overwhelming so it's not as hard to separate from the feeling in the next step of the exercise, but it's also fine not to. Just know that if you are having a hard time connecting to the inner adult in a minute, that is probably why and totally normal.

Are you able to locate it in your body? It's okay if you can't, but it's helpful if you can. If you can't, just try to get as specific as you can about what you're feeling. Either way, imagine pull-ing that energy out of your body and putting it about six feet in front of you.

Now take a breath and put your hand on your heart or give yourself some kind of loving touch. This activates oxytocin, sometimes called the love hormone. Studies have shown that oxytocin brings a feeling of self-love into the body. It's what mothers experience when they nurse and what we feel when we cuddle with someone we feel safe with. I'm asking you to do this because we want to be as centered as possible with the inner adult and feel compassion for whatever part of you comes up.

After doing this, ask yourself, *how do I feel about the energy in front of me?* Spoiler alert: this energy is an inner child part. It might be in the role of an inner critic, but it is your inner child. You don't have to see it as being in a body, though. In fact, even after all this time I still see it most of the time as an energy blob. But it still works! Some people see it as a color; other people see it as a person, right down to what they are wearing. And sometimes it appears as an inanimate object. Seriously. I have had people see everything from a dirty dish rag to an enormous building (more on that one later). However this happens for you is correct. You're doing it right! I promise.

Here's a tip: if that part is angry and you feel annoyed with it, you actually are merged with it. If that part is sad and you feel scared or sad, you are merged with it. This is where it gets a little tricky, because sometimes if that part is sad and you are annoyed or judging it, that means the inner critic is the loudest voice at that moment. Remember, the inner critic and the inner child often come as a team. But either way, you are not in the inner adult if you are matching or judging the inner child's feelings.

If you feel compassion or even neutral or curious about that part, then you are good to start communicating with it. But if you're not there yet—in your compassion or genuine curiosity—take a breath and imagine that part is taking a step back or you are taking a step back. Then check in again: how do you feel about it? If you still feel annoyed or angry, then try it again, and if that still doesn't work, ask it to step aside and bring that angry or annoyed feeling up and out of your body like you did in the beginning. Sometimes the inner critic needs our attention more than the hurt part of ourselves, so we need to talk to them first.

Once you are rooted in the inner adult, you want to get to know the inner child. You want to know more about it, what it needs from you, what you need from it, and what overall will help to integrate it. Here are some questions to consider:

- **What do you need from me?**

- **What do you want me to know about you?**

- **Where did you get your information about how you are acting or feeling right now?**

- **Do you trust me?**

I find it best to start with either what they need from me or what they want me to know right now. After that, you can start to get to know what else might help build your connection.

Keep in mind that your intention from the inner adult should always be about feeling compassion and how you can help this part feel safe in a way that feels good to both of you. So if you find yourself shifting from that perspective, simply notice and come back to the inner adult. Often just taking a breath, putting your hand on your heart, and asking the part to step back can bring you back.

After you have connection and the inner child feels safe with you, it's good to make a commitment to checking in. One of the many things I love about this work is that after you have made a connection, it can be a very low time commitment to keep it up. Most of us lead busy lives, and it can be hard to stick to a lengthy practice. It's tremendously helpful to have more in-depth conversations with your inner child and inner critic parts when you are triggered. But once you have done that, simply checking in to say "I see you" or "I'm here" is often all that is needed for a while to keep that connection up.

That said, just like with any relationship, if you told your inner child you were going to do specific things, it's important to follow through to earn trust. For example, if your inner child felt hurt because you never championed it or acknowledged your successes and you told them you would do that, you need to do that. Or if you told your inner critic you would be on top of keeping track of your bills and you don't do that, checking in to say "I see you" will be empty words.

The result of being in communication with your inner child should create more time, not less. Ultimately, feeling more self-compassion and integrating with them will free up time spent in self-criticism and help you to create systems and habits that will be more fulfilling and create more room in your life to enjoy it.

After you have done this, see what your inner child would like to do now. Would they like to go off and play? Is it like the client I mentioned earlier who has a more serious inner child who would prefer to sit at a desk and work? Or maybe your inner child would like to go jump in the ocean or go to another galaxy and explore a different world. They can do whatever they want to.

Since I am coming from an energy healing perspective, I believe that when we let these parts of ourselves do whatever it is they want to do, we are freeing up a part of ourselves and allowing our energy field to become brighter as these parts of ourselves grow and evolve. We are also releasing stuck energy, allowing space for new, more aligned energy to come in. We can only benefit from their adventures (or practical desk job). This is us freeing up energetic patterning and creating new pathways within ourselves that are aligned with our true desires and what supports us.

One last thing to note about this exercise: I have found it much more helpful to get to compassion, if you can, as opposed to only a state of curiosity, when you are talking to your inner child. Many times people mistake their analyzer for curiosity, but that is not actually connected to the inner adult. I see the analyzer as a little energy box just behind your sixth chakra in your head. Your inner adult is centered in your heart and takes up the rest of your body.

When we are in our analyzer, it could look like trying to figure the inner child out or trying to rationalize them out of their feelings. You probably make very good points, but that's not going to create connection. If you're genuinely curious—great! But if you can, feel some kind of compassion for your inner child. Remember, it's just a kid part of you that wants your love and wants to help you feel better, too.

Here's a transcript of what a session like this might look like. My client, Sidney, was working through feeling shame about not being there for her sister, whom she had to parent growing up. Their father was largely absent, and their mother was emotionally abusive, leaving my client to be her younger sister's primary caretaker.

I asked her to first locate the shame in her body and pull it out, putting it about six feet in front of her. She then took a breath and looked at the energy in front of her. I asked her how she felt toward her inner child (which was what the energy was), and she said she felt sad for her and all that she had been through, which is a form of compassion.

But almost as soon as she felt this compassion for her inner child, she very quickly heard a voice telling her that it was her fault for not showing up for this inner child that was carrying so much shame. This voice (an inner critic part) said that her inner child wouldn't feel shame if Sidney had done a better job of parenting her.

This was a complex wound for Sidney, because her younger sister—whom she was put in the position of parenting when they were both children—was mad at her for not taking care of her well as a child. So now, when Sidney tried to parent herself, she was immensely triggered when her inner child felt hurt that Sidney hadn't shown up for her. Sidney felt burdened and resentful at the idea of having to parent her inner child, too.

I have many clients who, although not in this exact position, feel exhausted by the idea of reparenting. They may have had to caretake others growing up, have children of their own, or have a lot of other responsibilities, and this feels like yet another thing for their to-do list. I completely understand this. The truth is, while it is some work, it is far less exhausting than living with an inner child that needs you and is being dismissed. This creates so much more inner turmoil and fatigue than the process of being connected and nurturing. But if you've had difficult experiences surrounding nurturing, of course it can be hard to feel like this time will be different.

Coming back to Sidney, she was having a hard time putting that critical voice aside, so I had her ask the wounded inner child if she minded stepping aside so that she could talk to the inner critic. Here is a transcript of our conversation:

Sidney: Okay, she said she was okay with that.

Natasha: Okay, great. Now can you locate the inner critic in your body?

Sidney: Yes, it feels like it's in my throat.

Natasha: Okay, so see if you can pull it out of you and do the same thing you did with the shame, put it about six feet in front of you.

Sidney: Okay, wow. She's huge, like an Empire State building size. Like a black shadow. Whoa.

Natasha: What? What's happening.

Sidney: I just think of like "whoa."

Natasha: Oh, okay. But she's still separate from you?

Sidney: Yes.

Natasha: Maybe we can have some appreciation for her. I have it, so I'm hoping you can. It's amazing, what this part of you did. It had to protect to you. You had no skills given to you as a child to care for yourself. It's as if you were given blunt objects to care for yourself. So what does she have to do? She has to get enormous to protect you. Because your mother was dark and destructive, and as a kid that felt to you like darkness. So this part of you took this darkness and multiplied it to help you. It's very creative. So anyway, how do you feel when you look at her?

Sidney: I'm in awe. Of how big she is. And she's . . . Actually, I'm looking up at a huge multistory building structure. And it feels like it's going to fall on top of me, like it's out of balance. I'm not scared. I'm like, whoooa, we need to do something here. You need some help? I'm in awe of how big she is. It's a building, not even a person.

Natasha: Ask the building: does it need you to know something? Or does it need your help? Because it looks like it's going to topple.

Sidney: She said, "Get out of the way. I need to fall over. I can't hold this up anymore. I need to fall over, without hurting anyone. I just can't hold it up anymore."

Natasha: I wonder what happens if you say "okay, I'm here. Topple over."

Sidney: Okay. It's like one of those kids' toys? Like building blocks that topple over. And it's actually kind of fun to watch it fall. It's entertaining. It just feels like relief that it's falling.

Natasha: How do you feel now?

Sidney: So, at the base of this tall building is this little . . . I hesitate to say it. She's a toddler. She's just like—she wants to play! She feels so relieved that I don't have to do that anymore, there's just this really light . . . well, I don't know. It's like there's two things going on. She's this little toddler who doesn't know what to do now. She's like, is she this cute little girl? Or is she this big scary monster building? She has no idea what is going on.

Natasha: Oh my God, this is amazing. So, can you tell her that she took on that role of the monster to help you, but that you are going to take care of her now? If that feels right to you.

Sidney: Yes, I can say that to her, but as I say that to her, I'm not frozen, but I'm looking around like, is this okay to do? I'm a little unsure of what . . . I'm not trusting. I'm not sure which part of me . . .

Natasha: Yes, you are merged with her. This huge protective system just fell down. So of course this part of you now is like "What the hell is happening?" Well, she's a toddler, so she didn't swear, but that's what she's saying. But what's important now is that now you are going to go into the process of finding what supports you, saying, "Okay, I'm not interested in talking to myself that way anymore. I want to be responsible in a supportive way." So it is a void in some ways. You did create this release, so you want to fill it in. But you can do that in the loving adult. You have those instincts. It won't be perfect, but you can go slowly and connect to compassion, just like you do with your dog and your son. You know what to do. You don't have to think about it; that comes naturally to you. But it does look helpful to contemplate how you are going to replace the negative self-talk. It looks important to contemplate that from a meditative or calm, grounded place. As opposed to analyzing it.

Sidney: Trying to figure it out.

Natasha: Exactly. Maybe doing that only when you are feeling calm and grounded, then considering that. Because it does look like you could get in your head about that, which might make it harder to connect to the loving inner adult.

Sidney: Right.

Natasha: Okay, and one more way to do this, to connect, is to tell her, "I'm so grateful for you, and I'm going to figure out the better way to handle things, and you can go play." It's okay if she's a little like "Are you sure?" You can say, "I'm sure. I'm the adult. I'm in charge. You go do you." And then check in during the day, or in the morning and night, even for five seconds. You can say, "I see you." Okay, so thank her and see if she needs anything else.

Sidney: Okay, I told her that I'm going to see her.

Natasha: Did she hear?

Sidney: Yes, she liked that. And now she would like to go play.

Natasha: Great. And remember, what that part used to do would fill the space that now feels like a void with what she imagined your mom would do. So as much as you can, find ways to fill that space with encouraging things. Maybe find quotes that are encouraging so that you have tangible things to turn to in those moments when you are starting to go into that negative self-talk. Or even "Oh, that part is coming up right now. Remember, you are a toddler. I can take care of this." Checking in with the adult and letting that toddler play instead of going into her technique for coping.

Sidney: Wow that feels like, wow, really, I can do that? It feels like a breath of fresh air, like I can do that? It's so bizarre.

Natasha: Yes, because that energy of harsh self-talk and big shadow negativity was a childhood pattern. In some ways it's all that it was. It's how she learned to cope. That pattern fell down. So when you are in the adult, in the present moment, you can choose a new pattern, a new way. Don't be hard on yourself as you are learning it. But you can learn it.

That was one powerful example of how talking to the inner critic can give you so much information and healing. And now that Sidney has that initial connection, it will make it easier to build even more intimacy with little check-ins.

This may seem like it would be hard to do on your own, but it doesn't need to be. I don't mean to minimize your experience if you are having a hard time connecting, just validating that it is truly possible for everyone to do.

Check in with yourself throughout the communication to make sure you are feeling compassion for your inner child. If you feel anything else, you are not in your inner adult, and you will be either managing that part or merged with it. All this means is that it won't be effective. It just takes some practice.

I have had only a couple of clients in all the time that I've done this process who have not been able to connect to their inner child with me initially. In both of these cases, it was because they were feeling stuck in the analyzer I mentioned above. The analyzer is great for practical day-to-day situations but incredibly unhelpful when it comes to finding solutions related to our emotions. In both cases, my clients were able to make contact with their inner child after that initial session; it just took little bit of back-and-forth between their heart and their analyzer. That was their habit, and they understood that it was something to be aware of.

Kids who grew up in trauma often feel safest in their analyzer until they develop a loving inner adult and can feel safe in their bodies. The idea of leaving our analyzer is terrifying, because as kids we felt if we could just figure out how to handle the situation when our caretaker was upset, we would be okay. Many times when we are "trying to figure it out," we are trying to figure out how we are at fault and how we are bad. We have an inner child part that feels inherently at fault and bad, and we are just trying to figure out if that's true or not. The truth is, it was never about our worth or what we did. It was about a parent who was making us feel unsafe emotionally.

Today, that can look like worrying about if someone is mad at us or if people don't like us, or reliving conversations to see if we said the right or wrong thing. This can feel terrible, but the idea of not doing that feels scary. It feels like there's definitely a solution but we just haven't gotten to it yet. The answer is in slowing down, taking a breath, and being in our bodies. This means feeling whatever feeling is coming up that we can't feel because we are analyzing. If we can feel the feeling with the support of the loving inner adult, we can move through it.

Of course, there are other reasons why we may feel like we need to figure things out. Ultimately it comes down to control. Those clients who had been merged with their inner child lived in their analyzers for so long that they couldn't contemplate separating from them.

Another reason why my clients couldn't separate was that they couldn't locate the analyzers in their body, because the analyzer was hiding in their head. That sounds a little odd, I realize, but when we are overanalyzing, we are hiding from our feelings, so therefore we are also hiding from our inner child. If the people I was working with could have brought out their inner children, much like the toddler hiding in the large building, they would have seen that they were scared and sad.

I have given you a lot of things to look out for, but I want to make sure you understand that it really can be simple. So much of healing and spiritual and personal growth comes down to being grounded in self-compassion and centered in the presence of that loving inner adult. Once you do that, you have perspective—you see possibilities that you can't when you are stuck in your inner child.

The External versus the Internal Inner Gaze

A last tip: I have noticed that when people were raised like I was, with their inner compass pointed toward a parent to please them, their inner child was often facing away from them. When I noticed this for myself, it was a game changer. If I'm feeling activated emotionally, I'll check in, and if my inner child is facing away from me, I'll let her know I'm here and ask her to face me. Doing this quickly changes her focus from the external need for validation to the internal, and I will quickly feel a shift in how I'm feeling. This is because I'm changing the trauma response of scanning the environment for threats or needing to get approval to being focused on the loving source of connection available right away.

Even if you can't or don't picture an actual child when you communicate with your inner child, you will likely get a sense of whether the energy is directed internally or externally. If you notice they are externally focused, encourage them to face you. If they refuse, don't force it. Feel the compassion you have for them and let it happen naturally over time.

Journaling for Connecting to the Inner Child

Another way to connect to the inner child is through writing. Sometimes people find it easier to get out of their heads when they write because it helps them feel less self-conscious. If this is you, journaling can be an excellent solution. You may find that sometimes you want to communicate with your inner child using one of the methods that I describe in this chapter, but that same method may not work as well on another day. Let yourself experiment with what works best at any given time, and try not to judge yourself if you aren't able to get the same results later. You definitely can, but it just may take some practice. For me, they all work, but sometimes I have a deeper connection with one technique than another at any given time.

You can start by feeling into whatever is coming up for you and then just writing without editing. As much as you can, give yourself over to what you are feeling, letting that part speak unfiltered. It may feel surprising or even funny when you let that part speak, as it will probably say things that are childlike. The inner child will often speak in absolutes. So if you are writing harsh things—like "I hate him! He's terrible! He's always like that!" or "I want to kill him! I wish he'd never been born!"—know that you are definitely merged with the inner child.

After you've let that out, take a breath and connect to the inner loving adult. Try putting your hand on your heart and taking in what you just wrote as if you were listening to someone who has just confided in you. And then respond from there. You can ask questions, you can encourage or nurture— whatever feels right. But try not to go into fix-it mode or talk your inner child voice out of their feelings.

Here's an example of how you might react to the same feelings from the perspective of the inner parent and the analyzer, respectively:

Inner Parent Example

Inner child: I'm really angry! Nobody ever pays any attention to me! I'm always getting overlooked!

Inner parent: You feel really angry. It's hard to feel overlooked. I'm really sorry you feel that way. I'm wondering if you can tell that I'm here and I am excited to pay more attention to you and build our connection.

Analyzer Example

Inner child: I'm really angry! Nobody ever pays any attention to me! I'm always getting overlooked!

Analyzer: That's not true, though. Remember last week when Megan called you to see how you were doing after that issue at work? You have lots of friends who care about you. You don't really have any reason to feel this way right now. Think about all the support you have.

On its surface, pointing out the support the inner child has seems supportive. And maybe after a connection is established and they feel heard, it would feel good to hear about all the support in their life. But starting with that is not really hearing them. You can try to avoid this by repeating back what they feel and offering empathy. If you can't feel that, remember that you are not in your inner adult.

You can continue from there, going back and forth until the process feels complete for you. At the end, thank that part for showing up and, like we did with the other exercise, follow through with any commitments you made to them.

I had a client who had a hard time hearing her inner child when she tried the first exercise in this chapter, which caused her to go into a self-critical mode. We were in a reading when this happened, and I got the information that she had a lot of pictures in her space coming from her inner critic that were saying, "You're terrible at this, you'll never do this right," and so on.

She had been a spunky, fiery kid, but that all got shoved down by the time she graduated from high school. She spent her whole life ignoring her feelings and focused instead on providing for her family. Providing for her family was wonderful, but her inner critic told her that she couldn't be connected to her true self and be productive at the same time. When she came to me for a session, it was because she could now feel her authentic voice wanting to come out. She felt stuck in her life, but she didn't know what to do next.

I told her that her inner child was not quite trusting of her yet, which is why she was having a hard time hearing her. I could see the inner child was very much there, but between being detached from her for so long and having a strong inner critic (who had gotten more attention over the years), it was hard for my client to hear it. I suspected that journaling would help.

After our session, she journaled and was able to bypass her inner critic by writing from her inner child's point of view— and her inner child was quite talkative! When I say bypass, I don't mean that in a spiritual bypassing way, where you shove the problem down and ignore it. I just mean that when she journaled, that part of herself was naturally more quiet. So if you're having trouble connecting in the first way, journaling may be a good way to go for you.

Chair Work for Communicating with Your Inner Child

Chair work is a term used in Gestalt therapy. The idea is that you embody and speak from the different parts of your personality as they come up.

1. Put two chairs or cushions opposite each other.
   Feel into the feeling you are having as the inner
   child. If you are having difficulty with this, feel into
   your body and see where it's located. Sometimes
   that helps to access it if you are feeling stuck in
   your thoughts.

2. As the inner child, speak out loud what you are feeling. Let yourself let it all out.

3. Switch chairs. Then make sure you are connected as the inner adult. Put your hand on your heart, or bring in the feeling of the loving parent, or do anything that helps you connect to that place.

4. Now respond to your inner child. Remember to take in what they say and acknowledge it. Don't go 138 into fix-it mode.

5. Go back and forth like this until you feel the inner child is feeling much better or at least is aware that you are there and doing your best to establish a connection.

Once you get used to this one, you may feel comfortable doing it on the fly. I will often talk to my inner child or critic as I'm driving. I'll imagine them sitting next to me and have a conversation that way. Again, whatever works for you is perfect.

The Goal Is Integration, Not Fixing Yourself

Now you have three techniques you can use to connect to your inner child. I want to point out one stumbling block that you might encounter. After you get your inner child to trust you (yay—good job!), you may find that they are fine with *you*, but mistrustful of the world.

My client Julie had an inner child who had been in a perpetual state of hypervigilance because of her domineering father. When Julie talked to her inner child, her inner child was clear that her dad was no longer a threat and that she felt safe with Julie, but she didn't trust that someone wouldn't show up and hurt her. This was our conversation:

Julie: She's still standing around looking for a threat, even though she trusts me.

Me: What if you told her that you understand that? It sucks to be scared and having to live in fear all the time growing up, but that you are here for her now.

Julie: Okay. She relaxed. That helped, just having me understand her.

Me: Good. Sometimes that's all we can do, and that is enough. We don't want to get into a mindset of having to fix them until they are totally better. It can be healing enough to be witnessed as they are, seen in that moment.

I bring this up because although there can be great changes after communicating with our inner child, we should be careful about looking at ourselves as a project that needs to be completed. We are human beings: we get hurt or angry, we experience messy feelings, and we can't fast-forward through that.

Sometimes the most healing action we can take is to validate our inner child's feelings and simply let them feel it.

I hear so much from clients who want to get past feeling a certain way. It could be sadness, anger, anxiety, or just feeling stuck. This is essentially telling our inner child that we don't want them around. *This is us abandoning ourselves.*

I experienced a time period when I would wake up with a feeling of not being good enough. As soon as I opened my eyes, I felt weighed down, almost like I was failing from the get-go. More than anything, I just wanted this sensation to go away. I wanted to wake up and not feel it. But one day, I realized that this was me perpetuating my abandonment wound by wishing my inner child away. So instead of trying to will away these negative feelings, I opened my heart to them and had compassion for my inner child. I had tried to do this many times before, but it didn't work, because even when I was feeling sad for her, I also wanted the feeling to just stop happening! I wanted it—and her—to go away. Fully embracing her as a part of what I was feeling allowed it to transform.

Just like in any relationship, there are so many nuances to consider. Communication is sometimes messy, but if it's rooted in self-compassion, you can't go wrong.

Troubleshooting

Sometimes we communicate but we still can't seem to find our way back to the inner adult, or the situation keeps repeating itself. Here are some techniques in case you get stuck:

Can I Speak to the Manager?

If your inner child is in a protector or managerial role, it can sound a lot like what you may associate with a parental figure. This is because sometimes the protector sounds super practical and authoritative. This may sound like:

- **I need to go home to see my parents because that's what good kids do.**

- **I have to work another three hours because that's what people who are good at their jobs do.**

- **I have to work out five times a week— it doesn't matter that I am sick/tired/ overworked.**

- **I have to organize all the plans because no one else will.**

- **[Fill in the blank here] is the smart/ responsible/right thing to do.**

You may notice that a lot of these are driven by shoulds. It may feel like the truth, but when you check in with your body, you will likely have a feeling of rigidity. It might feel like it has a judgmental edge to it, like "Duh, of course I am doing it this way." Part of why it sounds so much like the inner adult is that it *is* often doing the "right" thing. The problem is that because its ideology is so rooted in what is right or wrong, it's not checking in with your inner adult to see if that's also in alignment with what you *need*. So if you find yourself doing something because you think you should, check to see if you have a strong inner child voice talking that is very rooted in the story of what "everyone" should do, or what the "right" thing is.

Ask How Old the Inner Child Thinks You Are Now

Another thing to be aware of is that sometimes your inner child, especially when they are in the protector role, doesn't realize that you are an adult. If you're finding yourself going over the same issue, do the exercise where you pull them out of you, and then ask them how old they think you are. I did this once and found out my inner critic thought I was fifteen. Because of that, she wasn't comfortable letting go of her hypervigilant state—she wasn't going to let a teenager be in charge! As soon as I told her my present age, she instantly relaxed.

Attached at the Hip?

The next thing to be aware of, if you keep coming back to the same inner child who is hurt or angry and not feeling better (or feels better in the moment but it doesn't last), is that there's likely another inner child part that is hanging out with them. Ask the inner child you've been talking to that is upset to step aside and ask if there's another one that would like to talk. You can identify it by getting in touch with whatever feeling is strongest at that time. That may sound like a loud inner critic, or it may be anger or sadness or any other emotion. If you are unsure, it might be a feeling of resistance, and that's important to talk to as well. It's a little harder to identify resistance, but that some-times manifests as a feeling of "meh," or if you pull it out of your body, it may look like an invisible wall. It could also be a general feeling of "this is stupid; this isn't working." Remember that every single feeling is needing to feel welcomed. Bring that feeling up and see how it goes.

Get Outta Your Head!

If you find yourself stuck in your head, unable to connect to your feelings or your inner child at all, prioritize getting into your body. Here are some ideas for that situation:

- **Breathe consciously. Take a big breath in, and as you breathe out, check in with your body. Can you feel your feet? Your legs? Your stomach? What sensations are you able to be aware of? What are you not able to be aware of? Then seen if you can identify any feelings with those.**

- Put on your favorite music and dance.

- Go outside and, if possible, walk barefoot.
  If not, just notice what is happening in
  your surroundings.

- Take a bath or a shower.

- Do an art activity that feels joyful to you.

The Higher Self to the Rescue!

Finally, if you find yourself stuck, it is often helpful to do a meditation to connect to your higher self. This can help remind you of the expansiveness of your true nature and bring you out of the myopic world of the wounded inner child. No offense, inner child! But it has a limited worldview, and the truth of who you are is much bigger than the reality of where it lives. Playing in the world of the higher self can bring its wider perspective into your reality.

CHAPTER SEVEN

Your Higher Self

The higher self is part of your soul and simultaneously lives in your body and on the soul plane. It is connected directly to Source, which some people refer to as God, Allah, Goddess, or whichever name you feel comfortable with. You could even say the higher self is your reflection or experience of Source, as it is a part of that energy. This means that this part of you is always aware of your highest purpose and essence, unaffected by programming that makes you believe you are less than who you are. This part of you has an unconditionally loving view of your life. It also is helpful in that it is something that you can integrate into the physical world, especially the more you become aware of it. If you are an atheist or agnostic, you may want to think of Source as the best or highest part of yourself, the part of you that, much like the inner adult, is acting from a place of compassion and connection to your greatest good.

When we work on developing the inner adult relationship with our inner child(ren), it is expanding our connection to our highest nature, because we are working on the practices of self-compassion and creating a loving witness. Those are both practices often associated with meditation and spiritual connection, something the higher self is very much in resonance with. In inner child work we use those tools in a more active, practical way than we might in meditation, and we are working on them to heal trauma and any and all emotional pain. But this is not the same thing as experiencing your higher self.

When we actively engage with the higher self in the way we will learn to in this chapter, we are still healing trauma, but we are doing it by connecting with the joyful, expansive energy of the highest energy available to us, as opposed to focusing on the trauma.

This can have practical and transformational effects on us:

- **Being able to act from a part of us that is beyond all childhood conditioning**

- **Knowing deeply that we are worthy**

- **Having a feeling of our energy being large and feeling confident in taking up space**

- ◆ **Seeing the bigger picture easily**

- ◆ **Feeling connected to our intuition (and spirit guides)**

- ◆ **Feeling connected to our heart, allowing us to more easily give ourselves and others love**

- ◆ **Feeling more gratitude for ourselves and also our lives in general**

- ◆ **And so much more!**

Even though we all have a higher self—so in that sense it's a universal experience where we experience what I mention above—it's also a very personal one. The way I experience it will look different from how you will. Just like how people who believe in God or Source energy have a similar way of knowing what that is, it's also very personal in terms of how it comes through for them. The higher self is connected to Source energy and knows you as both your past self (and all the lifetimes that involved) and your future self where you also exist. Having a connection to the higher self is a huge resource that can instantly help you feel more expansive.

One of the things I personally love about working with the higher self is that it helps me feel like a badass. And not just *a* badass, but *the* badass that I am. Have you noticed how your friends see you in a more expansive way than you see yourself, that good, true friends see us as who we really are? I have a friend who calls me "*Glamour* woman of the year." Apparently *Glamour* magazine has a feature where the magazine names a woman who was successful in a variety of areas in her life—an all-around inspiring woman. My friend thinks of me that way! Do you think in a billion years I would have ever thought of myself that way? Absolutely not. But when I connect to my higher self, I *feel* that way, and having my friend's reflection of me in this way helps me to remember that it exists and that *I* exist like that.

When my beloved cat Oakley passed away, we put him to sleep at home. I was holding him, crying as he passed, and I suddenly felt a peace come over me. In a session with my friend who does the kind of energy reading I do, I asked her if she could tell what happened when I felt that peace. (When I am too close to something, it's hard for me to see, so I had a hard time checking that for myself. See also: when merged with an inner child part, it's hard to hear your intuition or have perspective in general.) She told me, "He put a picture in your heart of how he sees you." Obviously, I started to cry, and then she said, "Wait, no, he said it's of how you really are." Cue more tears!

Can you imagine if we felt about ourselves the way the people and animals who love us the most see us? It is truer than the programmed way we have been conditioned to see ourselves. It's why they can see us that way—because they don't have the conditioning we got in childhood keeping them from seeing the truth of who we are.

It's also why we see our friends in a more expansive way than they see themselves. Why we can't see ourselves this way? If this *isn't* you, if you *do* feel your true badassery on the regular, please accept a sincere congratulations from me—I mean it! You are one of the rare few who has a sincere connection to the true knowing of the spectacular being that you truly are, otherwise known as—the higher self. (But even then, don't skip this chapter, because there are always more ways to connect to your higher self.)

It doesn't have to be rare to have this connection, though. If you came from an environment where your true self wasn't nurtured, or you were even encouraged to disconnect from it to please others, it can take work to deprogram those beliefs that kept you from your higher self. But it's totally possible, and one way to do that is to consciously and consistently connect to this true version of yourself. Doing this is something that can get overlooked in healing if we are focused only on the inner child wounds as we work on ourselves. That's important, of course (so important that I have dedicated much of this book to it), but if that's all we do, we miss the fun part—and it *is* fun! Sometimes when I'm working on my own growth I can get myopically focused on the pain. But we grow through joy, too. In fact, we can grow much more rapidly through allowing ourselves to experience joy than in any other way. We grow through getting to know our highest self.

When I do this, I am suddenly aware of how much I have been underestimating myself, because I, like everyone else in this world, truly contain all the polarities—confidence, expansion, radiance, and ease of the higher self, as well as the insecurities that I have been looking at to heal. It includes the most expansive, most badass version of myself. But if I'm not focusing on that badass version, I can't get to know it and everything that comes with it, and therefore can't access it. If I were to get all motivational coach on you, I would say that the mantra for the inner child would be "if you can't see it, you can't heal it," and the mantra for the higher self would be "if you don't know it, you can't grow it." We tend to hide the inner child wounds in our shadow so we can't see them. And we overlook or don't get to know our expansive higher selves, so that higher part of ourselves can't grow.

When we are in regular communication with that part, we can feel so much more at peace and grow so much more quickly than when we are identifying with any part of our ego (even the loving inner adult!). Of course, a loving inner adult who is kind and encouraging is extremely helpful for growth. But there's a certain fast track that we can get on when we're connected viscerally to our most expansive self. I'm not about fast growth that doesn't last, so I don't want to give any false impressions. We definitely need both the integration of the inner child that comes from feeling our feelings and acknowledging their experience *and* the expansion of the higher self that holds the wisdom beyond the stories of the inner child and their history. But when we do them together, it's transformational.

Intuition and Communicating with Your Higher Self

One of the most common questions I get as someone who communicates with energy of all kinds is "How can I trust my intuition? How do I know if I'm talking to myself or my spirit guides?" The answer is trust, practice, and deconditioning from a culture that teaches us we have to see something or it isn't real. *The language we use to communicate with our higher selves is often dismissed in our culture as our imagination.* And the tricky part is that as we are learning, or when we're merged with an upset inner child, sometimes it *is* our imagination. But as Albert Einstein said, "Imagination is more important than knowledge. For knowledge is limited, whereas imagination embraces the entire world, stimulating progress, giving birth to evolution." In terms of connecting to the higher self, I would say that by allowing yourself to go into your imagination of what that may look like, you can give birth to your evolution of connection between you and your higher self.

As you practice, you will start to recognize when you are forcing it and when you are having a true connection. In my experience, what we sense or hear when we are consciously connecting in this way is hardly ever made up. My connection to my higher self gets stuck only when I start to doubt. Then I can find myself going into "making it up" territory. It can also happen if I am in fear and too much in a scared inner child part to trust the connection.

The truth is that there is no separation between you and your higher self. It's just that you have been putting the focus on a different part (or, more accurately, parts) of you. It is you, and you are it. But most people have been taught that Source energy exists outside of ourselves and that it's delusional to think we can experience it or even talk to it. It is my belief that Source energy in and of itself is too big for us to experience all at once, but we *can* experience our version of it, which is our higher selves.

So how do we do that? Just like communicating with the inner child, there are many different ways to tap into the energy of Source, and in this case the ways are likely infinite. If you have already communicated with your inner child or inner critic, remember that it took a similar leap of faith to trust that what you were hearing was true. With things like spirit guides and the higher self, we can get in our heads when it comes to the gravity of talking to a higher power. When I first began this process, I started with spirit guides first, asking for help from my highest guides and angels. But even if you're reaching out to Source, the process is the same.

Journaling for Communicating with Your Higher Self

Many times the higher self and spirit guides don't communicate in words. You may sometimes hear words, but sometimes you will be able to know what your guides are saying just through their energy. One way to start to access this connection is to know what kind of Clair you have. The Clairs indicate different ways people tune in to energy.

Here are some:

- **Clairaudient (hearing words associated with the energy)**

- **Clairvoyant (seeing images)**

- **Claircognizant (having a knowing)**

- **Clairsentient (being able to feel the energy)**

There are more associated with all the senses, but in my experience, these are the ones used most by people to communicate with energy. So whichever one you are most tuned in to is the one you will likely also use to talk to your higher self.

I tend to feel, hear, and know.

I also see, but that is rarer. I have plenty of clients who mostly see, however—there is no wrong way. And of course you won't know which one you use until you practice tuning in to energy, and one way to do that is by talking to your higher self.

If you are going to journal, you can sit at the computer or with your pen and paper, take a breath, and ask your higher self for advice on something you are going through. When you are talking to your higher self or the guides that are there for your highest good, it will always feel peaceful and expansive. It will never feel scary or urgent. You absolutely can talk to your higher self when you are afraid, but you must take a deep breath and wait for the communication to come from what will feel like a different kind of energy stream than any kind of fear or urgency from the inner child.

Years ago a friend of mine was walking home late at night in Brooklyn, in the center of the street, where the streetlights shone. A man popped up in front of her from the dark edge of the street, holding a knife, and demanded she come to where he was. She said she felt a calm come over her and heard a voice (clairaudience) telling her not to go there. She just knew (claircognizance) that if she did, he would kill her. She also felt a huge wave of compassion come over her. She saw he was on drugs, and she felt overcome with empathy for his desperation. Seconds later someone else started walking down the street, and the man ran away.

I bring up this story not only to point out her Clairs but to highlight that even though she was actually terrified, her higher self (and likely guides) spoke to her in a steady, slow, calming way. In her case, it was heightened, so it felt like the compassion overtook her, but when you're just shooting the breeze with your higher-self bestie, it will feel more like a conversation.

Here's a snippet of what it looks like for me:

Me: I'm not sure what to do about the cats. They aren't accepting Jonathan [our new kitten].

Higher Self: They are figuring it out. It doesn't look like that to you, but they each have their own dynamics, and they need time to establish their new order. Try focusing on your bigger picture and letting go. What comes up for you is a need for control, but you would be better served by expanding your energy and taking care of the fear coming up.

Me: How can I do that?

Higher Self: Let yourself feel it, and allow what is to be, rather than resisting.

Could I possibly be more on brand than talking to my higher self about my cats? Here we are; I'm not fighting it.

Visualization for Connecting to Your Higher Self

Another way to access this connection is to think of a person you admire whom you really resonate with. This works because we contain all of the qualities that exist, so we contain within us what we admire, and they are reflecting back those qualities. I believe we are focused on whatever quality it is because that quality has been dormant in us and wants to come out. This is a way that our higher self communicates with us, telling us we can benefit from making contact with this quality in ourselves.

When I was fifteen, I was going through a very hard time. My mother at that point had fully rejected me, and I believed in the worst version of myself that she was projecting onto me. There was a girl at school who was two years older than I was and a total badass, complete with a leather jacket. She was somehow equally beloved by the girls and the boys, exuded confidence, and happened to be the ex-girlfriend of the boy I was obsessed with. She was everything I wanted to be and thought I wasn't—*thought* being the key word here, because we contain all the polarities, all the multitudes. I was just woefully out of touch with this particular multitude.

I won't bore you with the details of the months-long period when I envied her (although it is a great example of how envying someone is a good indicator that there's something you have within you that you aren't doing or becoming, so you covet it in them), but after she graduated, the feeling abruptly changed. Or, more specifically, I changed. I had a mindset shift where I decided boys were stupid and I was going to revenge-fully embody everything I admired about her.

Now, the revenge part wasn't the healthiest approach, but little did I know I was feeling my higher self intuitively, and, having been so out of touch with that part of me, I was craving this connection to myself in a massive way. Seeing these qualities in this girl awakened within me the qualities like hers that I already had. Yes, I was admiring that seemingly everyone either wanted to sleep with her or be her best friend, but more than that, I was hardcore girl crushing on the fact that she exuded confidence out of her pores—something I couldn't dream of experiencing.

But dream I did. This may sound creepy, but she had graduated, so I wasn't trying to be her friend or obsess about her. In many ways I wasn't focused on her specifically—I actually knew very little about her—but that wasn't the point. But I imagined what it felt like to have her confidence, only from my interpretation. I put the feeling of confidence in my body by embodying her walk and how she held herself in the world. I felt that within me. It awakened a connection to my higher self, because my interpretation of her was actually the qualities of my higher self that were offline but were awakened when I saw something like it embodied in the world. How she actually felt was likely very different, but that doesn't matter.

When I embodied those qualities, it's amazing how much changed for me. Yes, I did draw more attention externally, but internally I felt more expansive, more confident. I had a bigger picture of myself and what was possible for me. I cared less about what other people thought because of this inner connection. You could argue that I was embodying a part of myself that was not the higher self but more like a confident protector, and that is possible too. But this felt very expansive, and the revenge energy I had felt previously evaporated when I felt this solid connection to who I truly was.

Maybe you know that feeling of falling in love or being with someone who brings out qualities in you that you didn't know you had. Those qualities already existed, because they are part of your higher self that you can embody more of. I've never loved the expression *fall in love with yourself* because it feels cheesy, but when we awaken to qualities within ourselves that have been dormant, it can feel like falling in love with ourselves if we are willing to let go of the programming that says we can only feel that way with other people. Our higher selves offer us this gift. Often, we fall in love with people who have qualities that we think we could never exhibit. But as I've already spoiled for you more than once in this chapter, you already have those qualities. We are subconsciously attracted to them because we admire qualities within us that want to come out. We instinctively know that we possess so much more than most of us allow ourselves to access. But when you can connect to your higher self, you can feel it. It can feel like a homecoming to allow ourselves to feel parts of ourselves that we have cut off from.

You can try this yourself. Close your eyes. Breathe in light, and imagine a cord going from the top of your head (your crown chakra) to a bright light above you. Feel or sense yourself floating up into a bubble of light that contains you and your higher self.

Now think of a quality you want to embody but don't feel like you can access easily. If you're having a hard time with this, think of something you want. Let's say you want financial freedom. What is the feeling behind that? It might be what's baked into the expression: freedom. That quality of freedom is something that exists in your higher self. Or let's say you are feeling anxious about giving a speech at work. The quality you want to embody might be confidence or a feeling of accomplishment, like it's clear you are a professional and know your stuff. Again, that quality already exists within you, in your higher self. If you're having a hard time feeling it, though, you can think of someone you admire who embodies it. But if you already have a good sense of what that would feel like, stick with that.

Now, tune in to your higher self and ask it directly (remember that this is part of the process of building that trust muscle): "What would it look like for me to connect to this quality?" You might hear words, or you might just get a feeling. If you're in the flow with this, you can keep asking questions like "Can you show me a version of myself where I already inhabit this?" or "How can I embody this quality more fully?" Then follow that information. It might be breathing into the feeling and visualizing yourself making the speech while you feel that quality. Or you might get some ideas that you want to write down about an action you want to take to demonstrate that quality. It will be different for everyone.

If you want, you can also think about someone whom you admire (like I did with the girl from high school) who has this quality. Now see yourself in the bubble with them. Ask them how they access this quality within themselves. You may be surprised to hear what they have to say. I did this once with Oprah, imagining her as my inner parent. I was asking her how she prepares for big speeches. She showed me how she tuned in and made a conscious point to connect to her higher self and make herself bigger through this connection. She said to me, "I make myself be the most Oprah I can be." I'm not saying I was talking to Oprah's actual energy. But with my higher self, I was bringing in the energy of how I saw Oprah and let her talk to me. It was incredibly inspiring, because when I was going to give a speech in the past, I often got smaller and worried about what everyone thought of me. But she showed me how powerful it was to value the connection to your higher self above anyone else in that moment and give yourself power simply by valuing who you are. She then showed me imagining her energy getting huge and feeling safety in this connection to her higher self and to Source.

While I am an energy reader and have the ability to tune in to people's actual energies, you don't need this skill to do this exercise. I believe that when we are tuned in to our higher selves, we can get all the information we need to embody the qualities we are seeking, even as it appears in someone we admire. Just like when I was in high school, we sometimes need to think it's coming from someone else to believe it's possible for us to embody. We never have to take on foreign energy; the qualities exist within us already.

The exercises I shared here are just some ways to connect to the expansiveness of your higher self. But the ways to connect are as limitless as your higher self! It can be as simple as asking it to connect with you more or asking it for advice. But often we don't trust that it can be that easy, or that it's happening at all. Give yourself the opportunity to build trust, and you will receive so many gifts from it. Depending on where you are on your spiritual journey, it can take time to stop needing concrete "see it to believe it" evidence to know it's happening. You may get that, but at first it may be a matter of "feel it to believe it" or "hear it to believe it."

However or whenever this connection does happen, it is such a gift to your inner child. Whereas the inner child lives in the past, your higher self lives beyond space and time. When the inner child feels you connecting with them (and the "you" in this case may be the higher self or it may be the inner adult, which is grounded and compassionate but still part of the ego), they get an experience of understanding how many more possibilities they have than the ones they had in childhood. This is such a transformative gift.

CHAPTER EIGHT

The Inner Child
in Relationships:
Boundaries,
Codependency, and
Self-Compassion, Oh My!

I t is transformative to have a truly connected relationship to
your inner child.

But what happens when we add another person into the
mix? This is when our past programming around what we
deserve and how we have experienced or witnessed boundaries
being modeled comes into play. If we experienced boundary

violations as children, this is where our fear of setting them originated. However we processed our family dynamics around boundaries (and everything else) was downloaded at a young age and lives on in the inner child until we bring them into the present with what we know now as adults.

We can soothe our inner child when they feel upset, we can let them know that we hear them, and we can give them what they need to feel safe, but if we're going to change how we interact with people, we have to interact with people.

What are boundaries in terms of relationships? Boundaries provide the framework for you to shape your life the way you want it to look and feel. Boundaries are how you let your inner child know that they are safe, that there are limits to what you will and won't accept in your life, and that you are responsible for yourself and your emotions. They let other people know what you are available for. They let your inner child know what you will allow to use up your time and energy. You can't have room for what is supporting you if it's filled up with what isn't.

What a concept for those of us who come from families that push past boundaries like they're breaking through the finish line tape at the end of a race. They hear you say "I can't make it to your party" and view that boundary not as the end of a discussion but rather the beginning of a negotiation. They may say in a very annoyed manner, "What? You have to come. You said you would earlier!" As if someone changing their mind is an unheard-of concept. Depending on their level of agitation, that exchange could represent anything from an aggressive boundary crossing to guilt tripping. If instead they said, "Oh, that's a bummer. I'm really disappointed. I was excited to see you and wanted your help," that's them expressing their feelings. But acting like you have done something wrong is crossing a boundary.

One of the wonderful things that boundaries can do is preserve your energy and make it so that you are using it in the ways that most fulfill you. They can also protect you to make sure that you have enough reserves.

In terms of relationships, boundaries mean you get to choose and have the people in your life who support you. It doesn't mean you don't get to have anyone if you are stating your needs, which is what you may have learned growing up. In fact, you might find that the people who go away when you set boundaries are the ones who were not the best for you. When you are listening to your needs and taking action to support them (boundary setting), it means you get to have more love, not less.

In many ways, boundaries do not come naturally to many of us—and understandably so! If your parent got angry with you when you told them you needed something contrary to their needs, of course setting boundaries feels antithetical to your true nature. But I promise it isn't. In fact, boundaries are the very thing you need in order to experience your true nature.

The inner child struggles with the idea of setting boundaries because they are a kid. They likely think they will get in trouble, or someone will be mad at them or abandon them if you set a boundary. Or that if they don't help, they are bad or selfish. This is all from childhood programming, and it's a lot for a kid to handle. That's why they need you, the adult, to step in.

When someone is crossing an emotional boundary, it can look like the following:

- *Guilt tripping:* **You say you can't help someone and they say, "I don't have anyone else to help me. You're the only one." Or "Fine! I'll be fine!" when their body language and energy are portraying anything but. While I have a lot of compassion for people who may be alone in their lives, it is not my (or your) responsibility to be the person in charge of anyone's happiness. If you can help out, great! But if it's taxing to you, it's not your job to take care of someone else's life (unless they are your children whom you are literally in charge of). If you were raised by someone who was a people pleaser, or if you had to people-please to feel emotionally safe, this may feel harsh to you. If that's the case, it's time for you to talk to that inner child who feels the weight of this.**

- *Lashing out:* **Maybe you tell someone you can't do something for them and they**

respond with "Wow, you are so selfish!"
or "You are always disappointing me.
You never do anything for anyone." They
criticize, raise their voice, and so on.

- *Withdrawal:* Maybe when you tell someone
that you need space, they give you the silent
treatment or stop being in your life. This
is a boundary violation because you are
simply stating what you need and they are
rejecting you as a way to manipulate you out
of your boundary.

- *Physical boundary crossing:* It can be very
obvious if someone is being abusive and
harming you, but it can also be merely
annoying. You ask someone to scoot over
on the couch and they refuse. Or you tell
someone you don't want a hug and they
come in and do it anyway, dismissing your
needs. Or someone in line at the movies
gets too close. These are all examples
of crossing a societally agreed-upon
physical boundary.

You may want to think about what a boundary crossing
looks like for you. Many times we will grow up with consistent boundary crossing about certain things, so we think that it's normal and then don't question that we are allowing this boundary crossing now as an adult.

I had a client named Jackie whose mother would treat Jackie's body as if it were her own. This wasn't a sexual boundary crossing, but she would do things like wipe her face without asking or grab her hand in public when Jackie was a teenager and didn't want that, or walk in on her when she was changing and ignore Jackie's need for privacy.

My client hated this behavior but thought that it was just what mothers do. She had learned that she wasn't allowed to have a boundary around her body in most ways. She then developed a disdain for anyone who hugged or touched her platonically. When this happened, she would feel herself cringe and her muscles tighten. She didn't know why she felt this way, because she was a warm person who liked physical touch and wanted to be able to receive hugs or simple physical affection from her friends.

When Jackie remembered the ways her mother had pushed her physical boundaries, we pieced together that it wasn't so much the touching from her friends that bothered her, but the fact that she felt she didn't have a right to set a boundary around physical touch. This left her inner child feeling like she had no choice (because she hadn't had a choice as a child) and had to agree to it all the time.

Boundary crossing can be so layered and nuanced that it's not always obvious. The more you are in touch with your inner child, the more you will know the familiar feeling in your body when your boundary has been crossed. You might feel anxiety, a pang in your stomach, or a general sense of not being comfortable. This is vital information. Our bodies communicate with us through energy in this way, and it's every bit as important as listening to the words someone is saying when you are negotiating a boundary.

If you have dismissed what your body is saying to you and overrode that information in the past, it may take some time to trust that feeling. But understand that by trusting it, you are trusting your inner child to give you information about what is making them feel safe or not. That doesn't mean you have to do what they say they need every time. Sometimes our inner child thinks in dramatic terms, like "I want them to go away forever," but that's not actually what they truly want or need. Your inner child may think you need to do something extreme to protect them, but in reality it isn't necessary for them to feel safe. In that case, listening to them tell you they want to be safe is not the same thing as following through with whatever they say they need, like making someone who hurt them go away forever.

But it does mean that having a discussion with your inner child will help you figure out if they are reacting from trauma or actually getting information that a person isn't safe. If you are interacting with someone who is familiar in the sense that they remind you of a parent who previously crossed boundaries, it may be both. But if you can center into the inner adult, you can then discern if it's important to act on their behalf, or if it just requires you to reassure your inner child that you've got this.

If you're unsure, err on the side of setting a boundary. It's better to be overprotective at first than it is to continue to ignore your inner child's needs.

My client Jennifer once said to me, "I'm comforting my inner child and telling her how much I love her, but the people I date have never given back to me as much as I give to them. I tell them what I need, and they ignore it, and then I end up giving anyway."

Many times, if we are taking care of our inner child by listening when they feel unappreciated and taking action on their behalf, we will not tolerate external relationships that are imbalanced. The relationship Jennifer described was one where her boundaries were getting crossed when she said what she needed, and there was clearly something going on with her inner system that was allowing her to continue in the relationship even though these needs were not fulfilled. Let me be clear: I am not blaming Jennifer for her partner's actions. It is not her fault that he crossed her boundaries, and she was not attracting this to herself. She was tolerating it, and that's the part we needed to figure out the why behind.

When I looked at her energy, I saw that she had a nurturing relationship with her youngest inner child, who felt cared for. But her inner adolescent was angry and a fierce protector, shielding Jennifer from being aware of patterns keeping her in this relationship.

She did this by filling her thoughts and feelings with a lot of "dread" energy and "why bother, nothing works anyway" energy. She was also judging Jennifer for continuing in this pattern. The inner adolescent was keeping her from seeing what was going on, even though the inner child felt emotionally nurtured.

Because Jennifer wasn't directly talking to that part, and because she had merged with the "why bother" energy of the inner adolescent, she wasn't getting past the point of nurturing the scared part. So her relationship issues weren't being healed (from the inner child perspective) because she wasn't getting to the next layer of the inner adolescent, who didn't want her to be alone. And even more to the point, she felt strongly that nothing she could do would help anyway, so she was staying stuck in the relationship.

How could she know this? If you are caught in a cycle of having to soothe a lot, and it helps initially, but days later (or months later) it's not making much change in your outer circumstances, chances are there's another inner child part asking for your attention. It's so important to be aware of a judgy or "why bother" feeling, because many times that feeling is even stronger than those of the wounded inner child. We think we need to focus so much on the squeaky wheel of the wounded inner child, but actually the judgment part needs our attention more. We could think of this as an inner critic part, and in some ways it is. But it appeared as an annoyed adolescent.

This may sound complicated, and it is one step up from basic soothing. It requires some more in-depth communication, just like any relationship! It may just take a little detective work by asking something like "Is there another inner child here that would like to be heard?" or "Is there any part of me that I haven't listened to that would like to speak to me now?" If it's still the scared child part, you may want to ask: "Do you trust me?" It may be that you are saying all the right things, but that part doesn't trust you. We'll go over what to do when that happens shortly.

The "nothing works" tactic of the inner child is very effective for what it wants. It wants to keep you in the same cycle so you don't expand and go out of its comfort zone. If you are feeling this, you can know right away that this emotion comes from your inner child. It is not the truth: it's just that you are not in the inner adult. This is the sister belief to "There's only one way; you're just doing it wrong" and "I can't get specific on what the right way is, but let's just keep focusing on how you are wrong." Both of these tactics are signatures of the inner critic, which keeps you in a place of confusion and doom. It is very easy to get lost in this cycle, trying to figure it out and ultimately losing time without gaining solutions.

In both examples, it's an inner child part you are merged with, whether the inner child itself or the inner critic, which is a part of the inner child. But you are infinite and expansive and full of love, and there are always possibilities and routes to get you back to that truth. This is the truth of the inner parent and higher self: you can always access these parts of yourself, so you are never far from the truth of who you really are.

You can communicate by asking to speak directly to the part of you feeling dread, or you can ask your scared inner child if they can step aside if you've been giving them a lot of attention and it's not helping anymore. See if you can pull the part of yourself that is frustrated or angry or feeling dread out, and then talk to them.

If you are having trouble with this, move on to the next step: try to feel your feelings. Ask yourself, "What am I feeling?" If you are having a hard time figuring out the answer, that means you are stuck in your head, which is keeping you stuck in general. So take a breath and ground yourself in the physical. Start becoming aware of your body. See if you can feel your stomach, your feet, your arms. See if you can identify any feelings coming up as a result.

In terms of my client, once she recognized that she was feeling dread during her interactions with partners who didn't honor her needs, she immediately saw that her angry adolescent was mad at her for never setting boundaries. Her adolescent self was stepping in to protect her inner child because it had no confidence that Jennifer would do the work of protecting her herself. The "nothing works" Jennifer's inner critic had been relaying to her over and over again was like a foggy energy that was masking the anger of her inner adolescent toward the inner adult for not being there for her.

If you have been ignoring your inner child's needs for boundaries (or anything else), they may not trust you right away to start protecting them. This is especially true if you have had a situation like Jennifer's, where you have an inner adolescent who is pissed off. Even if you do everything they ask for, it's unlikely they'll say, "Oh great! Now I feel all better! I'm going to go take a nap; looks like you got this!" Just like in any

relationship where you haven't been present or have let someone down, it can take time to gain trust. And just like in any
relationship, the way to build trust is to show up consistently
and follow through on your promises. I have found that it takes
less time to gain the trust of your inner self than in an external
relationship if you are really following through—but it can still
take time. If this happens to you, know that it's totally normal.

Jennifer's inner adolescent needed to know she was serious about showing up, so my client asked her inner adolescent
what she needed. Her inner adolescent said she needed to know
that she would acknowledge when she felt something was off
with her partner instead of brushing it off. In the past, Jennifer
would feel hurt by her partner, and she would comfort the part
of herself that was scared and say things like "I'm sorry you're
hurt. That made you feel sad. I'm sorry." But then she would
push down any anger or feelings about the specific boundary
that was crossed and not do anything about it.

Together, Jennifer and her inner adolescent came up with
a plan where Jennifer would write down every time she felt a
pang that a boundary was crossed and then acknowledge it to
her inner adolescent. She then said she would make it a goal
to bring it up to her partner, and if he pushed past the boundary, she would make it another goal to build up her inner adult
strength to draw a hard line.

Jennifer had anxiety about doing this, which is why she
would brush any conflict aside after she dealt with the sadness. In her mind, if she acknowledged the anger, then she

would have to take action. This is a really important point, so I'm going to emphasize it: *I don't believe everyone has to make changes immediately. In fact, this fear of having to take action once you acknowledge something isn't working is what prevents many people from knowing their own inner truth.* If they deny it, then they don't have to act. But it's extremely harmful to ignore what your inner child is telling you. This is what cuts you off from your knowledge, intuition, inner connection, and resilience. If you think you can't handle something, denial is not the solution. Being aware can be the bridge to getting you to the point where you feel like you can do something.

Sometimes the inner adult isn't developed enough, and it's threatening to the nervous system to do things like quit a job or break up with a person when you don't have that inner support yet. If you give yourself the grace to admit what you know to be true without forcing any action yet, it can give you time to build up an inner nurturing system so that you have more of an inner support system when you do make big changes.

I told Jennifer that the more she focused on what she needed instead of what the reaction to her boundary would be, the more it would help the process.

Let me be clear: I'm not saying to never take action. And there are times when waiting is not safe. If you are physically threatened by inaction, for instance, you're going to have to make the break first and build up the strength as you go. And you can do it. You *will* do it. But if you feel better going slowly when it comes to less dire situations, that's totally fine.

In Jennifer's case, she eventually would have to take action if she wanted to feel connected and aligned with her true self. At some point it will not be enough to hang out in the area of listening and not setting boundaries for yourself. Building trust in this way can start with hearing, soothing, and validating, but at some point, circumstances will require action. The more you are grounded in that loving inner adult and have connection to your higher self, the easier it will be. You will see the full picture instead of the one-sided, myopic version of the inner child. Remember, the inner child can't see the whole picture the way your adult self can.

Help with Setting Boundaries

Pen and paper (or computer and keyboard) are your best friends for boundary setting. When we feel anxiety after setting a boundary, it's often because we knew we needed them and set them when we were in our inner adult, but we retreated into our inner child after. We might say, "I got weak and went back to him/agreed to go to that party/took on more than I wanted!" and think that we failed to enforce these boundaries even though we were in the adult part of ourselves, but really we failed because we merged with our inner child and thus weren't able to stand behind them. So write down your boundaries and the reasons why you want them, so that if you merge with your inner child, you can read them and feel reinforced.

My client Deborah is a copyeditor who raised her rates but almost immediately went into a downward spiral of fear and a lack mentality when she tried to approach her existing clients with them. She had been exhausted by working for the rates she had been charging and knew she needed more money to continue to give her all. This was her setting a boundary with herself and her clients around what she was worth and what she would accept. To keep herself from spiraling and going back on her decision, she wrote down a list of reasons why she needed to raise her prices.

1. Raising her rates made her feel energized and more available for her clients.

2. She felt depleted by working hard for her old rates.

3. She felt like her rates reflected her worth.

4. Charging more money per job would give her more time for her other projects.

5. This change felt in alignment with her needs and wants.

That's it! When she felt like walking back her decision to charge more per job, Deborah would look at this list because it reminded her of her inner adult/higher self energy, and she felt more centered and realigned with her decision. You can do this for any decision you are wavering on: not visiting parents for the holidays, not taking on more work, committing to a new habit (that's setting boundaries with yourself around what you want to bring in or do less), and so on.

Make sure that when you create goals for yourself, you do it from your loving inner adult and not from an inner critic or inner child part. When you are not in alignment with the inner adult, you are trying to meet a goal that is not aligned with your true authenticity—for instance, dieting to be a certain size under the auspices of "health." You may have planned that goal when you went down an Instagram comparison hole, and then the process of meeting that goal became a constant dance between berating yourself for not having willpower and feeling happy with "wins" that were centered around an external ideal.

Another great resource for boundaries is energy healing. Remember in the beginning of this book how I talked about how much energy healing changed my life? Feeling my boundaries energetically gave me the foundation and structure to create them practically in my life. I talked a lot about grounding in that chapter, and that is definitely part of it, but another great tool is calling your energy back to you.

When I am planning to set a boundary and I'm worried that someone is going to react poorly to it, the first thing I do is call my energy back to me. I imagine a big sun above my head and call my energy back from where I've left it. I feel, see, or sense the energy going into the sun and see any energy that isn't mine burning away. Then I imagine that golden light filling my whole aura. This is my highest energy. At that point, I sense the boundary around my aura and make sure it feels nice and secure. When I'm talking to the person whose reaction I was afraid of, I might check in with myself to see if I still feel my aura secure and my energy with me, and if not, I'll call it back to me. Even if I can't tell, setting the intention to do so helps me maintain a sense of ownership over my space.

You can also visualize a shield of light around you that can't be penetrated by anyone else's energy. Make sure that when you set the intention to do this, it comes from a place of neutrality or even compassion—not defensiveness.

When we set boundaries in general, it is more about shoring ourselves up with our own energy than it is about pushing other people out. When we are in the pushing-people-out mindset, we can get into a power struggle. The more you can avoid that, the more you will feel centered in your own energy. This falls under the same category as this truth: boundaries are not an attack. They are about affirming your needs, not attacking someone else's.

If I feel like another person is getting into my energetic space, I might find a way to separate their energy from mine. Someone getting into my space might feel to me like being drained, finding that something doesn't make sense for me but feeling it anyway, becoming spacey and disconnected, or all of a sudden assuming responsibility for the person who has pushed past my boundaries.

A quick way to separate someone else's energy from your own is this: After you've called your energy back to you and filled yourself up with light, imagine a ball of light about five feet in front of your aura. Imagine it sucking this person's energy from your space. Then imagine the ball exploding and sending this person's energy back to them while your energy goes back to you. Then fill up with light again.

You can also picture the ball of light and put an image of that person's name or their energy in it, and explode the ball that way. Even though *explode* sounds aggressive, it's really not meant to be. It's just energy leaving, and the more it's done from neutrality, the better this exercise works. If you are coming from a place of trying to control the other person, it defeats the purpose of this visualization. You don't have to do this perfectly, so try not to get into your head. Simply having the intention to do it from neutrality will help a lot.

I talked a lot about boundaries in this relationship section because, other than being seen and validated, this is the thing our inner child craves the most from us. This is at least partially because boundaries are the actionable way we show our inner child that we see them. We may have caretakers who were not the best at showing us how to be in relationship with others and care for ourselves at the same time. Go at your own pace, exercise as much self-compassion as you can, and know that your intention to care for your inner child is the most important thing you can do when you interact with others in the external world.

CHAPTER NINE

The Inner Child and Narcissist Abuse

Before I delve into healing from narcissist abuse, I want to address what narcissist abuse is and why it can be considered offensive to use that term. This is such an important topic, and inner child healing is incredibly helpful in recovering from this type of abuse. My intention is always to help in the most inclusive, least judgmental way.

Narcissistic personality disorder, or NPD, is, according to the Mayo Clinic, "a mental condition in which people have an inflated sense of their own importance, a deep need for excessive attention and admiration, troubled relationships, and a lack of empathy for others. But behind this mask of extreme confidence lies a fragile self-esteem that's vulnerable to the slightest criticism."

Narcissism itself is on a spectrum and most people display some narcissistic traits at some point in their lives. When someone displays all of the traits listed above, that's when someone may be diagnosed with NPD.

Because NPD is, in fact, a mental condition, I want to address the idea of being a victim of someone else's mental condition. Doing so could appear to be insensitive, because someone with a mental disorder should not be pathologized or criticized for that fact alone. But the difference between NPD and many other mental health conditions is the *way* it manifests in relation to other people. The condition is often expressed through behaviors that are abusive and cruel, such as shaming and bullying. These kinds of behaviors aren't signifiers in many other mental disorders. Additionally, because people with NPD experience such intensity when criticized, they have a very hard time looking at themselves in a way that will create change, and often they have little desire to make changes in themselves. This creates a cycle where they often won't own up to the abuse they inflict on others, and therefore it continues.

I am not speaking of *all* narcissists when I speak here. There are people with NPD who are in therapy, seeking treatment and taking responsibility. But unlike people who have a mental illness such as depression or anxiety, when someone with NPD is *not* seeking treatment, their behavior is often pointedly harmful to those around them.

Behaviors such as gaslighting and triangulating are hallmarks of untreated narcissism and can make victims question their reality. For this reason, I think it is vital that I call out what is happening for what it is: narcissistic abuse. Putting a name to it—particularly when the victim has been told by a narcissist that they are making up what they are experiencing—is very healing and important for the person experiencing the abuse. Children of caretakers with untreated NPD often have been taught to question their own truth from birth. They have been trained to make themselves smaller and to caretake their parent by putting the parent's feelings before theirs. Naming it as abuse is a way of taking the power back by saying, "This is what happened, and this is what it is."

I had a visceral experience of how validating it was to name the abuse that happened to me. When my mother died, my sister and I went to my parents' house to help our dad go through her things. He told us, "You are going to find her diaries, and I don't want to see them because she could be vitriolic."

We did find her diaries, and she was, in fact, extremely cruel; a lot of her abuse was directed at me starting when I was about eleven. I won't repeat exactly what I found there, but if you're anything like those I confided in, you might feel bad that I read the horrible things my own mother wrote about me. However, you don't have to worry, because, first of all, it was my choice to read it. Most important, it was one of the most profound healing experiences of my life.

Reading through my mother's diary entries from the time I was born through my high school years, I felt an enormous amount of relief wash over me, and a huge sense of validation. *I hadn't been making it up.*

All those years, when my mother would deny she was judging me, deny she was telling lies about me to my family, deny how she felt about me in general and blame me—everything I felt was happening but kept getting gaslit about—it was all proven true in those diaries. The sense of having my reality affirmed was greater than any pain I might have felt from what I read there.

Another enormous benefit of the diaries was reading them with my sister. My mother had told her terrible things about me her whole life. You may think, "Why did she believe them?" But when two siblings are pitted against each other, often the result is that they don't think to question it. In our case, it was part of the family dynamic in a way that just felt normal.

After reading the diaries, my sister told me how sorry she was that she had believed our mother. Because she read them, we were able to have a relationship for the first time since I was eleven years old.

I bring this up to underscore how important it was for my healing to understand the context of what happened to me. The abuse I experienced was because of my mother's narcissism. Being explicit about that was part of getting my power back.

One last thing before I get into it: the reason this chapter is in a book on inner child healing is because inner child healing is particularly helpful for healing this particular kind of trauma. As you know by now, the wounded inner child is paused at the moment of a trauma. One of the unfortunate results of being a target of narcissist abuse is that it cuts us off from our intuition. Luckily, inner child healing is designed to help us reconnect. The tools at our disposal include the following:

- **Using the technique of seeing with our internal gaze and encouraging our inner child to orient their attention to us, rather than to the external world**

- **Connecting to that young part of ourselves with validation and assurance from our inner adult**

- **Cultivating self-compassion and giving it directly to our inner child, who was told they weren't worth it, and reminding them how it feels to connect to the truth of our inner adult**

These are all potent ways to get us out of the trickery of gaslighting and back to our intuition.

Gaslighting

Gaslighting is a very common tactic used by people with NPD, although it is not limited to them. We are at a point in our culture where "gaslighting" has become a common expression, but it gets misused often enough that I'll explain what it is first. It originally came from a 1938 play, *Gas Light*, in which a husband attempts to make his wife doubt her own perception and reality by slowly turning down their gas light every night and denying that it's happening when she asks him about it.

Gaslighting is emotional abuse, and when done consistently, it can create a huge chasm between our inner adult and our inner child. When we are gaslit, we begin to doubt our reality and merge with the wounded inner child who is afraid or sad, making it harder to feel our wise, secure inner adult. This condition is always reparable, but the separation between our inner child and our inner adult is painful and creates confusion. Emotional abuse is just as bad as physical abuse, and when we are being gaslit, we are already questioning whether what we're experiencing is really happening, or we are doubting our interpretation of it. That adds a layer of complication in terms of being able to heal the damage. You can't heal from abuse if you are also denying that it's happening.

The National Domestic Violence Hotline says, "There are a variety of gaslighting techniques that an abusive partner might use." Here are the five categories they mention, with my comments and thoughts about them.

1. WITHHOLDING
This is when the person gaslighting you withdraws emotionally.

After you bring up something you're upset about, you might hear something like: "I don't want to talk about this. You have no reason to be mad. I'm going to bed." They also might withhold affection or give you the silent treatment when they're mad, without giving you an idea of what you might have done to make them angry. This puts you in the position of questioning what you might have done, with no concept of what the problem might be, not to mention how you might resolve it.

2.   COUNTERING
This is when the person gaslighting you questions your memory or your explanation of events.

This could look like: "I never would have done that; that's not something I do." Or: "You always exaggerate. I never did that." When this is done repeatedly over time, especially when it is done to you as a child, this makes you doubt not just your experience of how things happened but also your intuition in general.

3.   BLOCKING/DIVERTING
This is when the person gaslighting you attempts to change the mood or tries to make you doubt yourself.

You might hear: "You are so crazy how you come up with these things; you're so easily influenced by people." Or, if you say, "Hey, can we talk about last night? I'm upset about it," they might respond, "Do you want to go out to dinner tonight, just you and me?" This is especially confusing when someone has been withholding affection.

4. TRIVIALIZING/ACTING CONFUSED

This is when the person gaslighting you minimizes or demeans your reaction to what they have done.

"You're still upset about that? We already talked about it; why are you still talking about this?" Or, "My last partner never cared how late I stayed out. Why do you care?" This is gaslighting, because they are trying to make you feel like your reality of *not* being over it is wrong or shouldn't be happening. It can send you into confusion about why you aren't over it, because clearly you should be (according to them). The reality is that they don't want to deal with your feeling upset with them and take responsibility, so they are trying to get you to ignore how you feel.

5. FORGETTING/DENIAL

This is when the person gaslighting you seems to have amnesia about what you're talking about.

When I was a teenager, I would often spend a long time fighting my mother, trying to make the case that whatever she was upset with me about wasn't actually my fault—and sometimes I would actually convince her I was right! She would say to me, "You should be a lawyer because you are so convincing!" (Never mind that often what we were arguing about was unfair to me to begin with.) I would always walk away feeling exhausted but also slightly euphoric that for a rare moment my mother accepted me. But *every time this happened*, I would walk back into her room anywhere from a few minutes to a couple of hours later, and she would be just as mad at me as she was before the conversation. This is an example of the intense "forgetting" gaslighting technique. Of course, this can also look like straight-up denial: "That never happened," "You are crazy," "I never had sex with that woman," etc.

Gaslighting Yourself

One of the effects of being raised by a caregiver who often gaslit us, or experiencing it for an extended time in a relationship, is that we will then do it to ourselves.

Here are some things you might say when you are gaslighting yourself:

"I have no reason to feel this way."
This is when you are letting another person's narrative be the determiner of *your* truth. When you have the inner adult

present, you can take a breath and check in with what your view of the situation really is.

"Other people have it worse."

Other people are having a hard time so . . . you should, too? It doesn't make sense, but it does minimize your experience very effectively.

"I'm fine."

This is often said as a habitual response when you absolutely, 100 percent are not feeling fine. This is otherwise known as pushing your inner child's feelings down to protect other people's feelings.

"They didn't mean it."

This is where we not only give the other person the benefit of the doubt, but we also excuse their behavior. Gaslighting ourselves in this case involves pretending that our feelings shouldn't matter, because the other person is innocent by virtue of not having meant to hurt us.

"I'm too sensitive/insecure/needy."

This is a common one. When you have been used to having your feelings treated as though they are too much, you become used to pushing them aside. Ask yourself: are you too needy, or do you just have needs that the other person can't or doesn't want to meet? That doesn't make either of you bad; it just makes the relationship not the best fit for either of you.

Dealing with Blame

Blame is a central theme in narcissism. Narcissists look at the world through a black-and-white lens. People are either friend or foe, good or bad, special or repulsive. And when it comes to disagreeing, whether it's about who's going to pick up the kids that day or whether or not the other person hurt your feelings, it will end up being about who is to blame or who is not to blame.

In a healthy relationship, when someone is in conflict, the focus is whether needs are being met, as opposed to participating in the blame game. For instance, if someone's feelings were hurt because their partner came home late and didn't text, this is how it might look:

Healthy relationship: "Why didn't you text? I was starting to really worry." If the person says they are so sorry, they lost track of time, their partner might say, "This isn't your fault, but I got triggered and felt rejected when you didn't call."

Narcissist relationship: there could be some withholding of emotion, perhaps going to bed without speaking. If the person does say something it might be something like, "You obviously don't care about me. You're so selfish, you never think about me." They wouldn't inquire if something came up to prevent communication or talk about what they are needing.

Growing up with habitual blame reframes the question "What do I or they need?" as "How am I bad and how do I get back in the good graces of my caretaker so I can feel safe again?" As an adult, if you notice yourself feeling self-blame, take a breath and come back to the inner adult. Do your best to connect to self-compassion, and only when you are in that place, ask your inner child what they need. This takes the scenario out of categorizing yourself and into self-healing.

The Hypervigilant Inner Child

In my opinion, the inner child with whom it takes the longest to create self-trust is the hypervigilant one. This is the case at least partly because they were formed when their very survival was at stake, and they took on the job of being the lookout for danger. To feel soothed, they must feel totally confident that the inner adult is present most of the time, and they must trust that inner adult if they are to be released from their post.

People without the hypervigilant inner child may not love to have their life uprooted, but they also don't have a trip switch ready to go off at any moment, alerting them to potential dangers. They don't constantly feel the need to scan their environment for those who may not like them. This is totally possible for you, too. You absolutely can heal this part of yourself and make your inner child feel safe and calm, even after that trip switch is activated.

The hypervigilant inner child was likely created because you were emotionally and/or physically abandoned when your caretaker was unhappy with you. That part of yourself became a genius at figuring out how to read your caretakers and informing you how you needed to act to keep them happy. The word *empath* gets thrown around a lot these days, but many times empaths are created from this type of trauma. When you are forced to be on alert to your caretaker's needs to feel safe, you develop the superpower of being able to feel what they are feeling.

Unfortunately, until those with hypervigilant inner children start healing, this part of them is often "on," and even though they might be excellent at reading other people, they give more value to this information than to their own feelings. In addition, this hypervigilant part is attached to their activated nervous system, so they will be hearing things through the lens of fight, flight, freeze, or fawn. It's very important for them to sound the fire alarm just in case anything *might* be wrong, so that they aren't caught off guard. The problem is that it leaves them constantly on high alert, which makes it very hard for them to connect to their soothing, loving inner adult.

One reason the hypervigilant inner child is harder to heal is because it can feel impossible to get them out of the mindset that their safety is dependent on something external working for them. They think that if a given person isn't mad at them, they'll be okay: if their boss recognizes their work, if they arrive safely at their destination, if their partner is never unhappy with them, they'll be okay. But the truth is, they really just need to feel the safety of their inner adult.

The way to get things on track is to get back to your inner adult as your foundation. That way, you can make sure you are using the internal gaze as opposed to the external gaze. That hypervigilant inner child is very married to the external, so make sure when you are talking to them that they are "facing" you. Whether you feel that energetically or visualize it, coax your inner child back to a place where they are focused on you. Then you can get to the work of soothing them.

Because the hypervigilant inner child is often stuck in their head trying to figure things out, I have found that the most effective way to get the hypervigilant part to feel safer is through somatic healing. Here are some of my favorite techniques for this:

Looking around the room, notice every place or thing that feels safe, or unthreatening. That could be anything. Is your chair a threat? Your walls? It sounds funny, but truly registering that *Oh, that painting is no threat to me* is calming to the inner child who has been wired to look for threats everywhere. Remind them that you are here now, in the present, and there are so many areas and things that are unthreatening.

You can build on this by showing them things that make you feel safe: your pet, a book you love, a candle, a person you live with who makes you feel safe. Once again, give them the reminder that there are objects, people, and places that regulate you.

You can also change the scenery. It has been said that "motion moves emotion." I know when my kids were little and I got them outside, even for just a drive in the car, it changed their mindset. The hypervigilant inner child often responds to a change of scenery to coax them out of their vigilance.

Emotional Flashback

The last thing I want to mention in terms of recovery from narcissist abuse is the emotional flashback. This term was coined by the amazing Pete Walker, a complex post-traumatic stress disorder specialist, in his book *Complex PTSD: From Surviving to Thriving*. He writes:

> Emotional flashbacks are sudden and often prolonged regressions to the overwhelming feeling-states of being an abused/abandoned child. These feeling-states can include overwhelming fear, shame, alienation, rage, grief, and depression. They also include unnecessary triggering of our fight/flight instincts.

When I have emotional flashbacks, it truly feels like I'm experiencing the feelings of anxiety, abandonment, or alienation that I had growing up, but without the visual component associated with traditional PTSD. I haven't lost touch with reality and don't think I'm a child, but I may as well be a child, because I'm merged with my inner child and I feel those feelings as if they were happening in that moment. Walker recommends soothing yourself by saying, "This is an emotional flashback." Just that recognition will get you back to the inner adult and help your inner child know they are not in the past.

If you experience emotional flashbacks, try practicing the techniques I've mentioned in this chapter, as well as those in the rest of this book, which are designed to get you in touch with your loving inner adult. By doing this, you let your inner child know you are no longer in your childhood—you are here, now, in the safety of yourself.

I hope it has been helpful to learn about the reality of narcissist abuse. In the same way that verbalizing that you're having an emotional flashback can help to de-escalate its effects, it can be equally validating to name yourself as a survivor of narcissist abuse to heal from that abuse. Naming yourself as a survivor does not mean that you need to feel like a victim. Instead, it's quite the opposite: it can help you regain your power, because when you name what you have been through, it means that you are no longer protecting the person who hurt you by pretending what they did to you didn't happen.

The Effects of Gaslighting

Not Knowing the Difference Between Healthy Self-Questioning and Doubting Yourself

This is something that takes time to learn if you were raised to disregard your own opinions. It's healthy to question whether you did something that was hurtful in a relationship or made a mistake at work. It's not healthy to be in a frequent state of self-blame or of doubting your feelings. Getting used to the question "What does my higher self think?" is very helpful when this happens.

Habitually Blaming Yourself

When you have been blamed consistently, you will get in a habit of framing conflict or uncomfortable feelings by trying to answer the questions "Who is to blame?" and "Am I the bad one or the good one?" And likely, you will blame yourself reflexively. When I was twenty-one, I met my boyfriend's brother for the first time. After just a few minutes of knowing me, he said, "You know, not everything is your fault." Apparently after years of being blamed by my mother, I wore that energy like a security blanket. And I don't use that metaphor lightly. For survivors of narcissist abuse, it can feel much safer to blame yourself than others.

Feeling Empty/Alone/Not Knowing Who You Are

This feeling can come up a lot when you aren't placating or caring for the person with NPD. When you are raised to know your caretaker better than yourself, you likely will have to learn as an adult what you want, need, and feel. Inner child work is great for this. Getting to know what your inner adult feels like helps you start communicating with your inner child and begins the beautiful process of knowing yourself.

Feeling Like a Bad Person/Not Good Enough

This is a big one. I have seen so many clients who grew up with narcissist caretakers who feel like there is something wrong with them at their core. I have healed a lot from feeling like this, but there are times when I have an emotional flashback (more on that later) and suddenly experience that creeping, terrible feeling, like *I'm just not good enough.*

CHAPTER TEN

The Joyful Inner Child

I saved the best for last: joy. It is so affirming to be connected to joy. The reason the subject of joy is not in the beginning of this book is not because I'm a sadist, but because we often have a hard time connecting to this part of ourselves until our wounded inner child gains the trust of the inner parent. This is why you may find that the joyful inner child spontaneously emerges after you have done some of what I have discussed in this book. I have had so many clients tell me that they organically start changing their behavior after addressing inner child wounds: all of a sudden they begin doing the fun hobbies they had long abandoned, have more fulfilling relationships, and feel that they can express themselves better than they ever could before. Once they have integrated the part of themselves who has been criticizing them for how they spent their time, or once they have healed an inner child who needed more attention, they become free to enjoy their lives more. From there, they find themselves growing even more: they find it easier to set boundaries, prioritize more time with themselves, become inspired, and feel more expansive because of this connection to their joyful inner child.

As I mentioned in the chapter on the higher self, you *can* grow through joy! In fact, this is where you will flourish most, as this is where your true nature—the essential part of yourself beyond childhood patterning and programming—exists. This is where we find out more about who we are and how we want to be in the world! But so often we will say this is the very thing we don't have time for.

I have to blame capitalism at least partially for this. Living in this culture where "if it doesn't make us money, it isn't valuable" makes us feel that we are wasting time if we are doing the thing that makes us more alive. And sometimes that thing that brings us to life is a nap. What is more anticapitalism than a nap? And truly, what makes a child more ready to feel joyful than a nap?

Taking a look at how you value what brings you joy can be transformative. So avoid the following behaviors, because they can prevent you from experiencing your joyful inner child:

- Downplaying your successes

- Filling what could be an exciting time with anxiety and "what could go wrong?" thoughts

- Telling yourself you don't have time to do the fun things

- Ignoring intuition hits that lead you to activities you love to do

- Filling your time taking care of others and never prioritizing yourself

I have a dear friend who has two businesses that take up a lot of her time. She was meditating and heard from her guides that it was time to write the book she had been thinking about writing for decades. Instead of ignoring that impulse and talking herself out of it because of time or because she had "better" things to do, she decided to do it. She had no idea how to write fiction and didn't have a plot fully thought out when she started writing. And she had the time of her life! Oh, and did I mention that she wrote it in less than a month? Yes, it came pouring out of her because she was listening to her higher self and the joyful inner child that had been chomping at the bit to express itself. Somehow her schedule would open up or she magically had more time as she prioritized her book. And often she would write for hours without noticing. That's the beautiful thing about putting our energy where our joy goes: we often seemingly magically find we have more time, and the energy conspires to allow ourselves to create more as we make it a priority.

That said, my friend did have some tests come up as she was writing. If she had let herself get distracted, she wouldn't have continued down the effortless road of writing a book that brought her so much creative fulfillment.

Here are some temptations that she avoided by noticing them and choosing to put her focus back on her book:

- **Worrying about what would happen after she finished it**

- **Worrying about where the story was going ahead of time**

- **Chastising herself for spending time "just" having fun**

- **Comparing herself to other writers**

- **Reading other books and comparing hers to those**

- **Reading about the mechanics of writing when it was going fine as it was**

And this wasn't easy! Her first impulse was to do all of those things. But she noticed, talked to her inner child parts about what they were feeling, recentered, and kept writing.

The creative fulfillment she experienced was a huge benefit, but there were so many other ways that writing the book helped her. Here are just a few:

- She felt more in the flow in her life in general.

- She felt more aware of when she was falling into old programming of "not enough," because she was prioritizing getting back to the joyful inner child.

- She was better able to see where in her life she wasn't feeling that flow, and the more she gave energy to the joyful part, the more that unflowing part stuck out.

- When it came time to promote the book, she was able to use the same "following the joy" energy and more easily get unstuck from worrying about everything that goes into that.

- It became more of a habit to check in with her higher self and guides, as that energy was more at the ready because she had been paying attention to that joyful part.

I used her as an example because it's so illustrative, but literally any time you make a point to follow through with even tiny impulses to do what you love, you are building this connection. When you do what you love and follow your desires, you know who you are at your core. This is the real you. What better way to grow than knowing yourself through expressing or doing what you love?

You can get there by that magical duo of mindfulness and self-compassion. Simply notice: "Oh, I really want to go for a walk today." And then . . . do it! Or "I want to paint. I don't even know why. This is weird; I haven't painted since I was seven." And then . . . paint! This is a hugely beneficial act of unearthing who you really are and bringing that person into your own consciousness. And imagine how many more parts of yourself you haven't met! You can meet them every time you take interest in what you love to do and give it a chance to live in the world— your world.

This is where self-compassion comes in. If you don't always follow through, that's okay! Be kind to yourself about it. Any amount you listen is better than pushing these feelings aside.

I encourage you to start. Start listening to the desires and impulses coming from a part of you that may have been long buried underneath the programming that says you aren't enough. I have met many people who have believed more in the "not enough" programming than in that perfectly worthy child underneath it. But I have never met anyone who wasn't completely and totally more than enough. I look forward to more and more of us making contact with the "more than enoughness" that is our true self. And I hope this book has helped you in finding your way there.

Acknowledgments

I am so grateful for everyone at Union Square & Co. who has worked on this book, especially my insightful and supportive editor Kate Zimmermann. I could not have asked for a more easeful experience. It means so much to me to have the opportunity to put this work into the world.

Everyone deserves a cheerleader like my fervently supportive, tirelessly loving BFF, Laura Bahr. I'm so grateful to you. And to all of my dear friends that are too many to name here, please know I see you and know the impact you've had on my being more of who I am.

I am an entirely different, better, more fulfilled version of myself since parenting my kids, Jamie and Kristina. I hope you always know how loved you are. Our home, including all of our animals, has redefined what family means to me.

This book is a product of learning to love myself and that is in no small part due to my husband, Brett Christensen. You always see the best, highest version of me and are an example of unconditional love. In many ways, this book is a love letter to you.

Last but not least, to everyone who has come to me for a session or taken my classes, I get to know my inner child better because of each of you. I am grateful to be on this journey together.

Index

A

Acting confused (gaslighting category), 187

Acts of service (love language), 71

Ajna (sixth) chakra, 45, 123–124

Alpha brain waves, 84

Analyzer, 34–35, 123–125, 131–132, 135

Auras

  boundary setting and, 178, 179

  energy healing and, 31–35, 38, 178, 179

  expansion of, 32–35

  giving away power through, 29

  spirit guides and, 36

B

Berne, Eric, 2

Blame, 77–78, 190–191, 196

Blocking (gaslighting category), 186–187

Boundaries

  auras and, 178, 179

  energy healing for, 177–179

  inner adolescent and, 169–175

  inner child and, 19–20, 164–170

  inner critic and, 113

  inner parent and power to set, 64,
    70–71, 72–73, 78, 93, 95

  inner parent and problems with, 53, 58, 59

  physical boundary crossings, 166–167

  for relationships, 162–170, 175–179

  for spirit guides, 36–37

Brain waves, 84

Bridges, Jeff, 80–81

Bullying, 61, 94, 181

C

Capitalism, 199

Chakras

  about, 44–45

  energy healing and, 32, 41–45, 99

  inner critic healing through, 110–111

primary chakras, 44–45

  first (root) chakra, 41–42, 44, 110

  second (sacral) chakra, 44, 45

  third (solar) chakra, 44, 45, 110

  fourth (heart) chakra, 44, 45

  fifth (throat) chakra, 44

  sixth (ajna) chakra, 45, 123–124

  seventh (crown) chakra, 45, 158

Chapman, Gary, 71

Claiming your energy field, 36–37

Clairaudient, 153–155

Claircognizant, 153–155

Clairs, 153–155

Clairsentient, 153–155

Clairvoyant, 153–155

Codependency, 28–32, 41, 192–193

Communicating with inner child,
  117–144

  about, 18–23, 117–119

  chair work for, 137–138

  external versus internal inner gaze, 133,
    184, 193

  goal of, 138–140

  journaling for, 133–137

  meditative connection, 119–132

  troubleshooting, 141–144

Complex PTSD: From Surviving to
  Thriving (Walker), 194

Co-regulator, 66–67

Countering (gaslighting category), 186

Creativity, 44, 45, 47, 200–202

Crown (seventh) chakra, 45, 158

D

Denial (gaslighting category), 187–188

Dissociative disorder, 14

Diverting (gaslighting category), 186–187

Doubting yourself vs. self-questioning, 17, 196

Doyle, Glennon, 80–81

Index

E

8 C's, 47
Einstein, Albert, 151
Emotional flashbacks, 194–195, 197
Emotional worms, 18–19
Empaths and, 30–31, 51–52, 192
Emptiness, 197
Energy fields. *See also* Energy healing
    about, 24–25, 26
    aura and, 32–35, 38
    claiming your energy field, 36–37
    clearing, 107–109, 111
    of family line, 107–109
    light and, 39, 108–109
    open energy fields, 29–30
    trust, 34
Energy healing, 24–45
    about, 24–30, 123
    auras, 31–35, 38, 178, 179
    for boundary setting, 177–179
    calling energy back, 38
    chakras and, 32, 41–45, 99
    claiming your energy field, 36–37
    empaths and, 30–31, 192
    of family energy, 105–109
    grounding, 40–43
    of inner critic, 105–109, 111
    light and, 38–39, 108–109
    mindfulness and, 33
    of narcissist abuse, 196
    self-compassion and, 33
    of self-doubt, 39–40
    separating from someone else's energy, 179
Expansion of aura, 32–35
External inner gaze, 133, 184, 193

F

Family energy, 105–109
Fawn mode, 67–68, 84, 192
Fifth (throat) chakra, 44
Fight mode, 67–68, 84, 192
First (root) chakra, 41–42, 44, 110
The Five Love Languages (Chapman), 71
Flight mode, 67–68, 84, 192, 194–195

Flow in life, 202
Forgetting (gaslighting category), 187–188
Fourth (heart) chakra, 44, 45
Freeze mode, 67–68, 84, 192, 194–195

G

Gas Light (play), 185
Gaslighting, 182, 184–190, 196–197
Gaslighting yourself, 188–190
Gestalt therapy, 137–138
Gifts (love language), 71
Gilbert, Elizabeth, 80–81
"*Glamour* woman of the year," 147–148
Good-vibes-only culture, 79
Grounding, 40–43, 47, 51, 175
Grounding cord, 41, 42
Growth
    description of, 87–89
    higher self and, 150
    inner adult and, 132
    as a spiral, 11, 73, 89
Guilt tripping, 164, 165

H

Heart (fourth) chakra, 44, 45
"Higher Love" (Winwood), 92
Higher self, 145–161
    about, 145–150
    communicating with, 151–161
    for communicating with inner child, 144
    journaling for communicating with, 153–155
    visualization for connecting with, 155–161
Hyperreactivity, 47–48
Hypervigilance, 48, 49, 139–140, 191–194
Hypnotic state, 84–85

I

Imagination, 151
"I'm fine," 189
Impulsivity, 54, 200, 201, 202–203
"I'm too sensitive/insecure/needy," 189–190
Inner adolescent, 169–175

Index

Inner child, 1–23. *See also* Boundaries;
  Relationships
  about, ix, 4–6
  boundaries and, 19–20, 164–170
  connecting with, 18–23, 117–144. *See
    also* Communicating with inner
    child
  defined, 1–4
  as embodying critical parent, 103–105
  healing of, 24–45. *See also* Energy
    healing; Higher self
  hearing or seeing, 101
  inner critic and, 97, 99, 103, 113,
    114–115
  inner parent development, 12–13, 14,
    18–19
  integration with, 6–11, 138–140
  joy for, 198–203
  in managerial role, 141–142
  in multiple-part psyche, 2, 13–14
  overreactions, 9–12
  in protector role, 141–142
  relationships and, 162–175
  in shadows of psyche, 15–17, 111–116.
    See also Wounded inner child
  visualization of, 1
Inner critic, 94–116
  about, 94–100
  boundaries and, 113
  connecting with, 100–103, 104–105,
    120–121, 124–128, 130
  healing of, 105–109, 110–111
  hearing or seeing, 101–102, 104
  inner child and, 97, 99, 103, 113,
    114–115
  naming, 100–101
  relationships and, 171
  reprogramming, 104
  shadows and, 111–116
  shame and, 112, 113–114, 116,
    124–125, 126
Inner gaze (compass), 133, 184, 193
Inner parent (adult), 46–61
  AWOL signs, 52–55, 56–58
  boundaries and, 171, 174–175, 176–177

boundary problems and, 53, 58, 59
boundary setting and, 64, 70–71, 72–73,
  78, 93, 95
compassion and, 55–56
connecting with, 92–93, 119–122,
  123–125, 128–132, 134–136, 138
as co-regulator, 66–73
development process, 12–13, 14, 18–19
embodying process, 52, 58–61
emotional flashbacks and, 195
exercises for accessing, 82–83
gaslighting yourself, 188–190
higher self and, 145–146, 150
hypervigilant child and, 191–194
invitation to, 73–79
journal prompt to connect to, 90–91
narcissist abuse and, 185
for narcissist abuse healing, 184
qualities of, 47
real-world examples, 80–81
reprogramming the subconscious,
  84–89
role of, 46–52
support signs from, 62–66
Integration, 6–11, 138–140
Internal Family Systems, xii, 47
Internal inner gaze, 133, 184, 193
Intuition, 41–42, 53, 64, 147, 151–152, 184
It Didn't Start with You (Wolynn), 109

J
Journaling
  for communicating with higher self,
    153–155
  for communicating with inner child,
    133–137
  for communicating with inner parent,
    90–91
  on shadows of psyche, 116
Joyful inner child, 198–203
Jung, Carl, 5, 15, 111–112

K
Kintsugi, 96
Kübler-Ross, Elisabeth, 56

Index

L
Landon, Michael, 40–41
Lashing out, 6, 10–11, 102, 165–166
Light, for energy clearing, 38–39, 108–109
Love
    inner parent and, 59–60, 62–63, 81
    language of, 71, 91, 158–160
    meditation and, 21, 22, 23
    narcissist abuse of, 9–10, 11, 28
    self-love, 71, 72, 73–79, 158–160
    ways to give and receive, 71
Love hormone, 120
Love language, 71, 91, 158–160

M
Managerial role, 141–142
Mayo Clinic, 180–181
Meditation
    brain waves, 84
    for higher self connection, 144, 146
    for inner child connection, 119–132
    for reprogramming childhood
        experiences, 21–23, 84–85, 86–87
    visualization and, 85–86
Mental illness, 14
Mindfulness, 33–34, 50, 203
"Mom globes," 54
Mr. Rogers, 40–41, 66, 80, 81
Multiple-part psyche, 13–14

N
Narcissist abuse, 180–197
    about narcissistic personality disorder,
        180–184. *See also* Narcissistic
        personality disorder
    blame and, 190–191
    emotional flashbacks and, 194–195
    gaslighting, 184–190, 196–197
    gaslighting yourself, 188–190
    healing from, x–xi, 11, 183, 195
    hypervigilance and, 191–194
    of love, 9–10, 11, 28
    triggers and, 9–11
Narcissistic personality disorder (NPD)
    about, 180–184

    blame, 190–191
    emotional flashbacks, 194–195
    gaslighting, 184–190, 196–197
    hypervigilant inner child and,
        191–194
National Domestic Violence Hotline, 185
Neediness, 189–190
Neuro-Linguistic Programming, 43

O
Obama, Michelle, 40–41
Oprah, 40–41, 80–81, 160
"Other people have it worse," 189
Overreactions, 9–12
Oxytocin, 120

P
Paul, Margaret, xi
Peace, 43, 79, 82–83, 148, 150
Physical boundary crossing, 166–167
Physical touch (love language), 71
Physical touch, for connecting to inner
    parent, 92–93
Positivity, 79
Posttraumatic stress disorder, 195
Primary chakras, 44–45. *See also* Chakras
Protector role, 141–142
Psyche
    multiple parts of, 2, 13–14
    shadows of, 15–17, 111–116
Psychic Horizons, xi
PTSD, 195

Q
Quality time (love language), 71

R
Racial injustice, 60–61
Reactive feelings, 9–12, 20–21, 47–48
Relationships, 162–179
    boundary crossings, 162–170
    boundary setting for, 175–179
    inner adolescent and, 169–175
    inner child and, 162–175
    inner critic and, 171

Index

Reprogramming
  childhood experiences, 21–23, 84–85,
    86–87
  inner critic, 104
  of subconscious, 84–89
Rogers, Mr., 40–41, 66, 80, 81
Root (first) chakra, 41–42, 44, 110

S

Sacral (second) chakra, 44, 45
Safety, 84–87, 222
Second (sacral) chakra, 44, 45
Self-blame, 77–78, 196
Self-compassion, 6, 33, 132, 146, 184, 203
Self-doubt, 39–40, 48
Self-love, 71, 72, 73–79, 158–160
Self-questioning vs. doubting yourself, 196
Self-trust, 191–194
Seventh (crown) chakra, 45, 158
Shadows of psyche
  inner critic and, 15–17, 111–116
  journal prompts for, 116
Shame
  emotional flashbacks and, 194–195
  inner critic and, 112, 113–114, 116,
    124–125, 126
  mental illness and, 14
  narcissist abuse and, 181
  overreactions and, 12
  wounded inner child and, 15–16, 68
Sixth (ajna) chakra, 45, 123–124
Smells, for connecting to inner parent, 92–93
Solar (third) chakra, 44, 45, 110
Somatic Experiencing, 2–3, 66
Somatic healing, 66
Soul, 145–146. See also Higher self
Spirit guides, 36–37, 147, 151, 152, 153–155
Stress response, co-regulator for, 66–73
Subconscious, 84–89
Survivors of narcissist abuse, 11, 195

T

Tastes, for connecting to inner parent,
  92–93
Theme songs, 92

Theta brain waves, 84
"They didn't mean it," 189
Third (solar) chakra, 44, 45, 110
Throat (fifth) chakra, 44
Thumb squeeze, 42–43
Tolle, Eckhart, 73
Trauma
  defined, 2–3
  effects of, 50, 131
  emotional flashbacks and, 194–195
  empaths and, 30, 192
  external vs. internal gaze, 133
  higher-self for healing, 146–147
  posttraumatic stress disorder, 195
  wounded inner child and, 184
Triangulating, 182
Trivializing (gaslighting category), 187
True self, ix–x, 2, 20, 54, 149

U

Unconscious, 112

V

Vedas, 44
Victim-blaming, 60–61

W

Walker, Pete, 194
Winfrey, Oprah, 40–41, 80–81, 160
Winwood, Steve, 92
Withdrawal, 166
Withholding (gaslighting category),
  185–186
Wolynn, Mark, 109
Words of affirmation (love language), 71
Wounded inner child. See also Narcissist
  abuse
  about, ix, 4–6
  asking for attention, 17
  chakras and, 45
  healing of. See Energy healing
  in shadows of psyche, 15–17, 113,
    114–115
  shame and, 15–16, 68
  trauma and, 184

About the Author

Natasha Levinger is a trauma-informed inner child healing expert, spiritual coach, medium, and energy healer. Using a mix of an energetic healing model that involves the chakra system and other modes of therapeutic methods such as Inner Child Healing and Mindful Self-Compassion, she has helped hundreds of people to identify and heal core issues that were in the way of their being their most authentic and highest selves. Through her practice, Highest Light Healing, she sees wonderful clients from all over the world, teaches classes, offers guided meditations, and more.

She lives in the Blue Ridge mountains with her husband, two children, and a cavalcade of both adopted and foster cats and dogs.

You can find her on her website, www.highestlighthealing .com, her podcast, *Getting to Know Woo*, on Instagram and TikTok as @highestlighthealing, and as a regular contributor on www.mindbodygreen/wc/natashalevinger.